Believe!!

Inspiration ❧ Empowerment ❧ Motivation

CARLENE T. GLASGOW

WESTBOW
PRESS®
A DIVISION OF THOMAS NELSON
& ZONDERVAN

Scripture quotations marked (NIV) are taken from the Holy Bible, New
International Version®, NIV®. Copyright © 1973, 1978, 1984, 2011 by Biblica,
Inc.™ Used by permission of Zondervan. All rights reserved worldwide.

Scripture quotes marked (KJV) are taken from the King James Version of the Bible.

WestBow Press books may be ordered through booksellers or by contacting:

WestBow Press
A Division of Thomas Nelson & Zondervan
1663 Liberty Drive
Bloomington, IN 47403
www.westbowpress.com
1 (866) 928-1240

Because of the dynamic nature of the Internet, any web addresses or
links contained in this book may have changed since publication and
may no longer be valid. The views expressed in this work are solely those
of the author and do not necessarily reflect the views of the publisher,
and the publisher hereby disclaims any responsibility for them.

Any people depicted in stock imagery provided by Thinkstock are
models, and such images are being used for illustrative purposes only.
Certain stock imagery © Thinkstock.

ISBN: 978-1-5127-8685-9 (sc)
ISBN: 978-1-5127-8686-6 (hc)
ISBN: 978-1-5127-8684-2 (e)

Library of Congress Control Number: 2017906933

Print information available on the last page.

WestBow Press rev. date: 7/13/2017

ACKNOWLEDGMENTS

To my lord and savior Jesus Christ in whom I love honor, and worship. I say thank you Lord, for your inspirational gifts, and talent you have engraved within me which I do not take for granted. Thank you master God for holding my hands in the walk you have commissioned, and ordained me to do. You are an awesome wonder, and I thank you.

May you continue to open a Tsunami of blessings upon me as I step out holding on to the faith you have bestowed within me. May your assignment towards me continue to keep me humble, and grounded while delivering. Make me a Blessing Lord. I thank you.

To my blessing from God my wonderful husband and gentle giant Mr. Alanzo Glasgow. A man who stand for nothing less than the best, he stands for righteousness and justice, a no nonsense man who wears the qualities of excellence. His gentleness is amazing, and his heart is in the right place.

Alanzo compromises not when it comes to the word of God. He is a 200 percent God fearing man who remains humble without effort and I love you darling. Mighty man of valor. I thank you for all the years after God for being my support, and body guard when ministry calls me to different assignments. You never said one day you were to exhausted to assist me. In my travels you bless, and release me to head out where God leads me to minister. I appreciate you so much words cannot describe. Your encouragement and blessings after God for me to proceed with this book is enormously appreciated and I say thank you. A great mentor not only to me, but others. A man of great character, and I love you.

You held my hands 37 years ago as we walk down the isles, and I am extremely elated to say this is beautifully, and wonderfully perceived.

Thank you Al, and may God blessing, and the blood of Jesus saturate you with unlimited favor. I love you.

INTRODUCTION

There is an atmosphere that has consumed the hearts souls, and joy of some women due to the stress of everyday lives.

It is so sad to view the burden, hurts, and walking time bomb waiting to explode just by a prick of a mean word.

This book positions its arms around women who have the desire to make an impact in society, but just need that inspiration, empowerment, spiritual fulfillment, encouragement, and confidence that nothing is impossible with God

It challenges women and encourages them to discover their strength, gift, talent, and hidden ability. It tickle's women minds reminding them they can be a voice in society not an echo, provoking the brain of their uniqueness, and the assurance that they are beautiful excellent queens who has not yet completed their assignments.

Allowing their fragrance of kindness, and love to pave the way for the younger generation coming afterwards.

God is a restorer who can establish the works of your anointed hands along with your voices that leaves a legacy well sown into lives while imparting wisdom to great minds.

Take a minutes women and Selah("Pause".) You will definitely prove your gift is not constipated.

Just believe—persevere—step forward

And blaze in Jesus mighty name. Amen.

INTRODUCTION

There is an atmosphere that has consumed the hearts souls, and joy of some women due to the stress of everyday lives.

It is so sad to view the burden, hurts, and walking time bomb waiting to explode just by a prick of a mean word.

This book positions its arms around women who have the desire to make an impact in society, but just need that inspiration, empowerment, spiritual fulfillment, encouragement, and confidence that nothing is impossible with God

It challenges women and encourages them to discover their strength, gift, talent, and hidden ability. It tickle's women minds reminding them they can be a voice in society not an echo, provoking the brain of their uniqueness, and the assurance that they are beautiful excellent queens who has not yet completed their assignments.

Allowing their fragrance of kindness, and love to pave the way for the younger generation coming afterwards.

God is a restorer who can establish the works of your anointed hands along with your voices that leaves a legacy well sown into lives while imparting wisdom to great minds.

Take a minutes women and Selah("Pause".) You will definitely prove your gift is not constipated.

Just believe—persevere—step forward

And blaze in Jesus mighty name. Amen.

CONTENTS

CHAPTER 1

Run for Your Life

Most Holy of Holies!

Christians sometimes profess to be head tilt on one side with dress sweeping the floor, stacks of bibles of all translation, and sizes, also the biggest carry-on bag you have ever seen.

Let me say this, folks may try to fool the world at times, and believe they have gotten away with the deceit.

That might be your belief in the fleshy world you are living in.

As believers we ought to do what the word of God say we should do, and never try to apply some icing on the dirty act that are being portrayed.

Take off the mask and face the world undiluted and decontaminated, (Purged) yourself. Believers can be the example God has created us to be in the world.

If the world cannot place trust in us, then who will?

They will run for their life. We must be real, and not be a carbon copy of other persons anointing. Never practice someone else's signature, you will be exposed. God is gigantic, and he can be embarrassing at times, to a point where he can expose you to great extent.

If you recall for nearly two years Paul was ministering in the synagogue and at the lecture hall of Tyrannus, and throughout, where the people both Greek, and Jews heard the Lord message because they were extremely powerful words.

Have you ever wonder why Paul and Silas were so powerful that crowds, and scores of people followed them. I can answer that for you.

They were real not fake. They were filled with the Holy Spirit, desperate and hungry after the word of God in an unfiltered form.

We cannot duplicate what God has given to each individual, what is given to you is yours. If you recall, the power God gave to Paul was accompanied by unusual miracles, that the enemy knew the real from the fake. Don't ever try someone else's miracle for you might have to run for your life.

The powers that was given to Paul was so vigorous, that when the hand kerchief touch his skin it was placed on the sick people, and they were healed of their diseases, and evil Spirits within them came out.

That is the power of the true and living God.

This is where I am going to tell you, run for your life if you know you are trying to duplicate another, you will be extremely sorry.

Some Jews who were traveling from town to town casting out evil spirits tried to use the name of the Lord Jesus.

They were in for a surprise.

The incantation (Spell), they used was this.

In the name of Jesus whom Paul preaches I command you to come out - Acts 19:13

The Spirit was still waiting they did not move. These were the seven sons of Sceva a leading priest who were doing this.

I really hope they were fit and able to head this race that was about to take place.

They went ahead, and tried it on a man possessed by an evil spirit, and the spirit replied!

Get ready for this. ("Chuckle".)

The spirit replied I know Jesus and I know Paul but who are you?

He leaped on them and attacked, with such violence, that they fled from the house naked and badly injured (lol).

Don't fake it if you were not appointed.

Don't touch if it was not given to you, that is called stealing, that is high way robbery and the penalty is a very high cost.

The word of what happened spread quickly all through Ephesus to the Jews, and Greeks alike, and a solemn fear descended on the city, and the name of the Lord Jesus was greatly honored.

Many who became believers confessed their sinful practicing of magic, and they brought their incantation books which cost several millions of dollars, and burned them at the public bonfire, and the message of the Lord spread widely and had a powerful effect, all because the called and the chosen ones was appointed for such a time as this. It came with extremely very high consequences, which the evil seven was not willing to follow.

They wanted the Paul blessings quick, and right now, so they try to duplicate but they learnt their lessons very well through an exercise work out by the demon, who chased after them.

This showed them, and also us, that if we are not spiritually equip in knowledge, and strength from the Holy Spirit.

Run for your life.

Acts-19:15.

CHAPTER 2

At Midnight, One Moved On and One Stayed. (Naomi, Ruth, and Orpha—Ruth 1:16)

Did it ever occur to you what became of Orpha?

I taught so.

We never knew what became of her but we knew what became of Ruth.

Even though Naomi insisted they both moved on, Ruth was determined not to do so. Have you ever wonder why? I believe God had a plan so strong, it blinded her not to see what Naomi was saying to her, and deafen her not to here what Naomi was telling her to do, and it was all a set up from our master God.

Could it be that Ruth felt in her spirit, her future is there with Naomi.

Maybe she taught, where am I going.

She was so humbled, and loved by her mother-in -law that she did not care where Naomi was heading, she just won't let go.

Ruth said, where thou goes I will go, I will serve your God and these remarks spoke considerately. (Ruth 3-3:4)

In this modern day we are living, it is rear to find a daughter-in-law with such personality like Ruth.

We definitely knew it was all God plan. They both came to Bethlehem empty, Naomi lost her husband and two sons, Ruth lost her husband, and she did not want to return to her home town, could it be she had no future their, maybe it was extremely shameful for her to return to her town void.

She moved on with Naomi into a strange land, but who would have taught it would be strange for a little while.

They arrived in Bethlehem so empty that Naomi told the people do not call me Naomi anymore call her Mara (Bitter), for she have returned to Bethlehem empty. That sounded like a woman with a wounded heart.

Little did she know God was up to something.

Ruth was determined nothing was going to separate them. In life, when God makes a connection, that has a tag that say destiny, we are to hold on to it come what may, because you might just be a quarter of an inch away from your huge break through.

Ruth could have left as Orpha did when they exited Moab, after their father-in-law Elimelech death, but no, she stood on course in what might seem like a sinking ship, considering Naomi age, she held on for dear life refusing to erase the word conquer in her mind. When you are a woman called by God, and you are confident you will press through towards your destiny.

Ten years after Naomi husband died and her two sons Mahlon and Kilon died.(Ruth was a Mobite)

They arrived in Bethlehem at the beginning of Barley harvest, the owner of the field where the great harvest was taking place was Boaz who was Naomi's family. They focus on the positive, and what might be coming to them in Jesus name. They did not allow history to define their arrival to a new city.

Boaz was Elemelech relative Ruth father-in-law.

God through Naomi was setting things in motion now. She started to prepare Ruth to step into position. She told Ruth, go to Boaz field, and gather grains but go behind the harvesters, then Naomi bless Ruth, and send her forth.

In life there is a time we must start at the back and not get to pushy, stay at the back and wait for your next command, and do not be loud (sonorous) to get notice. Just be respectful and glean.

By then Boaz arrived at his field and after he greet his workers and Bless them, God put his focus directly upon Ruth without her being facety he ask the question, who is that girl? God is good.

His foreman filled Boaz In with the information, she was also working really hard in the field.

You must put your best forward honestly, and continue to do good, do right. Now look at this picture, Boaz first approached Ruth, and the favor started spilling all over her.

He told Ruth to stay with them in his field, he said to her do not go to other fields, that was very clear. Do not go is a key indication that God was present.

Boaz had to have seen, and feel something in Ruth for him to warn the young men not to interrupt her, or be disrespectful to her.

The Master had a mark on Ruth for kindness to rain upon her real good. Favor has visited her.

She got perfect treatment best of everything, even water they drew from the well. She was not treated like a reject.

Ruth was so over whelm and humbled she ask Boaz, why are you being so kind to me?

Knowing I am a foreigner. Little did she know dominion has visited her household.

He said, I also know the love and kindness you have shown to your mother-in-law, and he Blessed Ruth.

Wow. That is beautiful.

Be kind to your mother-in -law, your blessings are sure to reside in your presence.

At Lunch time Boaz called Ruth to dine with him she got food more than she could eat. Goodness and mercy followed her. After lunch God step up the blessings. She was allowed to gather grains right among the sheaves without them stopping her. They allowed her to pick up, and in her path they drop some bundles of grains along the way. Ruth were excited to get home to tell it all, I can see her walking and running along the road with joy and pure excitement. Ruth even took some left over lunch to Naomi. They talk and shared the days happening over dinner, and to top it of that day Boaz told Ruth to return and work until the harvest season was ended.

God had opened up a way where their seem to be none (Phil 2:13). Now its time for the next dimension.

Naomi told Ruth, tonight you will take a bath, put on perfume, and dress in your nicest clothes, and go to the threshing floor, and do as I tell you. This is a great example women can take pattern after, by being cute for when your husbands get home after a hard day's work.

Its time I find you a permanent home, go to the threshing floor after he have eaten, and lie down, uncover his feet, and lie there. he will tell you what to do next.

Ruth did not fight Naomi plans because she loved and trusted her so much, and the other thing was she lay prostrate at his feet, that is the humblest any one can be. The word of God teaches us, he that humblest his or herself will be exalted (Matthew 23:12)

Afterwards Boaz recognizes her at his feet and he was astonished, she identified herself in a still soft voice saying, I am your servant Ruth, she asked him to spread the corner of the covering over her feet for you are my family redeemer.

Then Boaz bless her because she was portraying family loyalty (Ruth 3:10).

Boaz even described her as a honorable woman, she did not runaround town looking for a younger man, she stood in the gap of maturity dignity and wisdom, that is a classy woman. Their was another man next in line to be king, who was a closer relative than Boaz, he would have to deal with that obstruction before proceeding with his plans for Ruth.

She were not afraid, because I believe she already knew what ever God had planned for her will materialize eventually in his timing.

So Boaz did what he had to do by morning. Ruth stay at his feet for the rest of the night until morning, but got up like the proverb -31 woman did.

She got up before light because God vision for her must be handled with prudence, she knew to keep that secret and not to let anyone know she was with Boaz.

I could see her joyful facial expression, and hear the tompting of her heart. As if the promises and the beautiful treatment was not enough blessings, he ask her to open her cloak and spread it out, he measured six (6) scoop of Barley and gave it to Ruth, Boaz then help her put it on her back and Ruth left towards her mother-in-law Naomi home. The number six in the spiritual is efforts and labor which tells me in life when you make an effort in your laboring God will bless you.

Boaz not only taught of Ruth, but of Naomi also that he did not want Ruth to go home empty.

My God. Favor did rain.

Ruth spoke off all that occurred that night, then Naomi told her now just be patient. I believe they both Todar God ("Lift their Hands and Give Thanks").

We must be patient in life, get things in motion and wait on the master (Set It and Forget It). The transition took place, and Boaz finalize what was needed to seal his passionate feelings towards Ruth. He got the right of way to marry Ruth

I can see cart wheels taking place in Ruth and Naomi home.

So Boaz married Ruth, and she moved into his home, he slept with her and she became pregnant and God Bless her with a son who they named Obed meaning (Servant Worshiper). Naomi took care of him, and the women in the town rejoice with Naomi knowing what a hard life she had, they even bless Obed saying may he be famous, and that he became.

Ruth was better to Naomi than seven sons, and that in itself is a huge blessing.

Naomi cared for Obed as it was her own, and at least she had a son again.

Obed became the father of Jesse, and grand father of David, and this is how the father deals with his chosen ones his children. Maybe Ruth, Naomi and Orpha left with one intention, and that was to head to Bethlehem. But God always see ahead, and he knew the plans he has for you (Jeremiah 29:11), so he allowed Naomi to throw out the plan and offer them the freedom to go their separate ways just to get Ruth and Naomi in one circle of agreement.

Orpha may have been a troublesome person in the long run so God set up the whole plan, to lay her down lightly and Orpha fell for it.

God knew the bond Naomi and Ruth had, and he already knew the future would be greater that they even expected due to the love and obedience Ruth had. When God is speaking to the heart and you listen, the outcome will be grand like Boaz Ruth and Naomi received because they listen to the still voice, and move by the spirit. Ruth was a humble, wise, respectful, obedient, God fearing, praying, fearless, bold, hard working, thirsty for approval from God, satisfying others, not a selfish kind of a woman, and for that God held her hands all the way, from a widow on a dusty road to a field then to a palace, and to me that's called favor from the most high God Lord and savior Jesus Christ. It is a lesson for us as women, that no matter what you might be experiencing or facing at present, i say put on the Ruth mind set and keep focus. You see, if she focused only on the situation, that would have crushed her spirit, but her eyes remain laser in at all times upon God. With open eyes she traced the price while keeping determination, not to miss the catch that was being thrown at her swiftly, and she was not distracted, she caught it in the form of Boaz. What a catch, that's victory.

Ruth received greatness from her womb. She and Boaz together begot Obed. What can be better than this?, Nothing. Women, you are more powerful than you think. I say stay the course, and never surrender in a haste, you can withstand to stand. Amen.

Perez father of Hezron Boaz-Obed
Hezron -Ram Obed-Jesse
Ram Amminadad Jesse -David
Amminadad-Nahshon Nahshon- Salmon Salmon-Boaz
Salmon married Rahab and made Boaz
Wow!
What can be better than this ending? Nothing.
This is totally God doing. Amen

CHAPTER 3

The Rain is Over—Change Position

The definition of the rain is moisture condensed from the atmosphere, that falls visibly in separate drops.

Their have been a soaking, and rainy season along the road, sometimes you slip and slide, but manage to maintain your balance and support, not to go down. When you have your feet planted on the rock, and persevere a good grip holding on to the Lord and Savior Jesus Christ everything will be alright.

This is something you must learn, and I guess you have proven this time and time again while residing in a comfortable or uncomfortable setting

While you are in a rainy season, you must be dressed for the weather while holding on to the word of God, keeping in mind what the word of God teaches us in Ecclesiastes, time and season change, therefore the rainy weather will not be everlasting.

It will definitely come to pass.

I realize while the weather of life sets us back for a little bit, or so it may seem we must not be caught unprepared like the five virgins were, (Matthew 25:1:13).

We must be ready at all times, and keep in mind change of

position is inevitable (sure to happen), some where along in your lives.

The confirmation is The rain is over.

Now we wait, for direction from the Master on what the next step will be. You must not be anxious or excited but remain alert vigilant humble and calm standing on God word and promises. You must have full trust in God, and God alone.

Man promises fail, but the master keeps his promise.

I believe this change of positions is a new season, that is shifting for the best.

We must be prepare spiritually, physically, and other wise, using wisdom.

This is a powerful word, and I am looking forward to seeing what GOD has in store for you. He never gives a word and fall back on his promises.

It may not come at the appointed time we desire it to, but I believe God timing is perfect. He holds the compass of life.

Know this and remember always, be anxious for nothing, he also tells us be not weary doing good, for in due season you will reap what you sow if we faint not. Galatians-6:9

Believe me, you will not faint especially with a word like this. We pray for God strength to consume us with power("Dunamis"), and vigor so we will excel in excellence, and perfection in all we do with the name of God before, behind and around us in Jesus name.

I believe in God, and to prove him daily is my desire, and it should be yours also.

The rain is over, and you are close to changing position, exercise your faith, it will be from a storm to the sunlight, from peace to obstruction, from rain to a tsunami, but guess what, God out stretch hands orders your steps.

He guided us with a pillar of fire by night in the darkest time, and a cloud by day to preserve us from the heated days, while conserving your energy

Sometimes that heat could distract us in an uncomfortable

way. But be mindful, and stand on the word of God as your support, and never give up.

The rain - A season of flood, land slide, thunder, lightening, high winds, hale, tornados, snow earthquake, a halt of running errands, Stillness, a soaking, slipping and sliding. But they all come to pass.

Change Position: From comfortable to shifting into a new position.

While preparing for your new setting and new season, rise up, and believe.

Shando, God will turn things around. he always does.

CHAPTER 4

Keep Moving

Sometimes in life their comes a wind of changes, and definitely in some folks personal life there is not just a change, it's a lot of changes that you know will come, and sometimes you tend to forget God word for a little while that was spoken into your life, and you laps into a mode just for a second.

Never the less life can take us for a stroll at times through the valley, and the mountain top for a few months, few weeks, few years or so.

What we must learn, while keeping in mind is that nothing last forever.

This lady was walking to work one morning in the rain and she said, a little tear came to her eyes when a car passed by and drove direct into a puddle of water that soaked her clothes and shoes, but she kept moving.

Another time in the blazing hot sun, about 94 degree that day she was moving one step at a time tired and the Holy Spirit said to her these words. Keep moving.

He explained to her, it may seem extremely hot, tiring, wet and overwhelming at timed, like you will never arrive to your destination, but remember these words, keep moving.

No matter how long the road seems ahead, it may even look

like you will never see the end of that leg of your walk just keep moving.

Don't worry, don't look around, keep focus, and know without a doubt you will arrive to your destination. You will arrive as long as you keep moving.

From their on it was a wake up call for her, that no matter what the situation is in your life, and I extend it to your families life also, just keep moving, and have confidence, you will arrive to your destination, and you will definitely touch the pinnacle.

I urge one and all no matter the condition and what ever it may bring along just keep moving.

Let your life be based on the keep moving technique.

When you feel like taking a pause along the way and giving up, remember keep moving.

When the road seems long remember keep moving.

When your job seems slow but you are still going daily faithfully, and committed to being their no matter if there is a client that day or not, remember to keep moving.

And when life throws a medicine ball at you, dodge that ball, and keep moving. The mistake you will make is to fall and stay down, and give up right in the middle of your victory. If you fall be sure its on the trampolines of life, and bounce up swiftly.

If you manage to fall along the way, get up, steady up, pop your neck left and right, and keep moving in Jesus mighty name. Amen!

I say to you, keep moving.

CHAPTER 5

Throw off Excess Baggage

Throwing off extra baggage, that would otherwise hamper a voyage, helps for a smooth and safe ride.

This was practiced by sailors long ago.

God sent a storm in, the ocean upon Jonah - Jonah -1:14, and he was punished, due to his disobedience.

He told them, to pick him up, and throw him over board, if they don't, the storm will not stop. (Acts 27:18:19). So the sailors did as they were told.

That is a revelation right there.

Sometimes you must throw excess baggage over board, and other times we got to change position, so the storm can cease. You must recognize what God is saying to you, and obey or you can be like a drowning man in an ocean with no fish to rescue you, and take you ashore.

Any person who deliberately choose to have a blinded eye towards what God is showing or telling you, can eventually feel the wrath of God, their and then he will definitely get your attention, be obedient, and do what God say to do, or you will have a well laid altar in the belly of the Fish, until the third day resurrection season.

This is the God we serve, the Fishes of the sea obeyed him,

and followed plans. They connected with God when it was time to make the next move.

When God wants your attention, he allows you to loose all hope in the attractions, and materialistic things of the world, that will turn you totally to him, not only in body but in taught, so that your pray shall be earnest.

Even the fishes knows the voice that ordered them. (Be still and listen to God voice). When it became time to spit Jonah out, Mr. fish obeyed. Jonah 1:17.

When the word comes from the master, you must be sensible enough to obey, take of your crown (earthly), and your robe, get into Sackcloth and ashes, and Step out of the seaweed that's wrapped around you like a knot.

At times God will put you in the belly of your situation, in the belly of trials, in the belly of rejection, in the belly of subjection, in the belly of humility, in the belly of silence, in the belly of spiritual building. Until you cry and bow to him

Until you pray earnestly

Until you surrender to God totally

God will order the jaws of the fish to open.

Closed doors will be open.

Physical blindness, and scales will turn into spiritual vision where you will see the light.

God will have pity on you, and his hands that was stayed on the cover, that was holding you back with fierce wrath of anger will be removed.

When you look on further, you saw where God speared the city of Neniva after they took heed, and obeyed, even the animals was ordered not to eat a mussel of meal, everything in there midst fasted.

We need to take pattern from this book of Jonah, and see the outcome of him, when he did not obey the master, and what the outcome could have been if he did. Something to ponder on.

God might very well be speaking to you as individuals. Keep your faith in God totally, and you will experience a spiritual revelation, in your home, family, neighborhood, and the world.

May God Bless you.

CHAPTER 6

Menopause Don't Have to Be an Issue When God is in Control

Genesis -17 - (The Laugh that Backfired For the Better)

A promise was given, and some where along the line it was determine in the human mind to be a joke (Humor).

Laughter was the first expression given. Although Abraham, and Sarah knew God, the first thing that came out was laughter.

I want to believe most times this happens to those who perceived to be born again Christians, who I presume know the word of God, and what it say. Those who are professing to be equipped with every verse of the bible but who's faith is in captivity by the devil. This is a trick from the pit of hell.

We are the ones who should be standing on the promises, that was given to us, we are to be standing in the gap as intercessors. But most time we get into the Isaac spirit which means laughter.

Abraham and Sarah was given to them a promise, and this was given to them by God, but they who were known to be so strong in the Lord laugh in their minds. I can see them now giggling away.

I would predict, the first thing should be coming out of their mouth, mind or heart should be to start thanking God for his blessings upon their life in advance, and that is why believers sometimes or should I say most times get left behind.

God at times speak to his children, and we laugh at everything.

We must realize, when God say he will do a thing, he stand on his word. His word is confirmation.

In Sarah and Abraham era where there was no experimental medicine, they would not have been able to conceive, and to top it of they were both in the prune stages, that's what we call dried up.

Sarah was already in menopause mode in man site, but not with God.

In the book of life its not that way. God promise them this beautiful son who will be taking up where Abraham left of, and it will be a Bless nation.

God had everything in order, he told them what baby they will have time of birth, and what to name the baby.

I am speaking on all women behalf who desperately are in need of a child. Menopause was never an issue then, and as long as you believe in God it should not be an issue. We know as long as it is the Lord will, it shall come to maturity, and if it did not then believe and know he has other plans for you. There is lots of precious children who desperately need to be adopted. Never the less as long as you stand on the promises of God he will never leave nor forsake you. He is and will always be there in every situation.

Your life is not at the end, when you see you are entering the menopause stage because Menopause is not and will never be an issue.

Before we get there, at times we need to be willing to have a name change, and be willing to Bow down to the Master in reverence, thinking not in disbelief, but by faith believing.

When God speaks to you respond, yes Lord without intent of doubt in your heart.

If you try to contradict God, he can at times leave until you are ready to relax let go, and listen. When the contraction comes breathe, and push. Push out your faith, push out your confidence in God, push out your belief, and relax as you get ready to deliver your Isaac. Let go and let God

Your spiritual insight of Laughter can be good when it comes to the promises of God.

Read and be Bless.

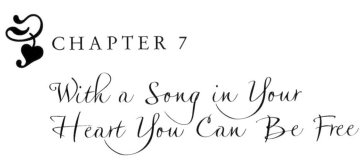

CHAPTER 7

With a Song in Your Heart You Can Be Free

Sometimes you might feel all bind up alone, and in captivity.

As we read in the book of Acts-16, Paul and Silas were thrown into prison for being men of God who carried the name of Jesus Christ wherever they went, and for that they were hurl into prison.

You may say the jailers were cruel, then you can say, the government of the city was with evil heart when you look at this in the physical.

Let us take a look at Paul and Silas case, they could have proceed with, the feeling of loneliness despondent and sadness all night long. But you know what? They turn the sadness in to joy, and the darkness into light, and instead of weeping all night they sang, and prayed with not a worry in their heart. Ask yourself this question?

Why? And how?

You may look at it this way saying, they had a song in their heart at midnight, yes they did, and we must learn to have a song in our heart at all times also, I can say this, they turn their sorrows into joy because they realize weeping may endure for a night but joy comes in the morning (Psalm 30:5). They recognize God never fail them in any situation before, and they knew he was not about to do so.

They knew God was not dead but he is alive, and they knew it was just a moment in time for God to come through. So they sat and sang, and when they were tired singing they prayed up a jail brake that set them free in the midnight hour.

What we saw happen was a domino saving effect, where the jailer and his family was saved, think about that and trace back your situation and predicament you are in now at present, and see if it can match up with two men who were suppose to be on death row but still sang. Two men who never knew if they will ever see family members again but they still pray.

Are you their yet?

No situation you are facing now can compare to Paul and Silas imprisonment. God is the battle axe, and weapons of war, Jeremiah 51:20, who fights on your behalf at all times. Just call out to him.

I want you to stop what you are doing, put down the laundry, get on your knees, and start thanking God for not giving up on you. When life challenges seem rough start praying for restoration in your life, and for your household, and I guarantee, God will see you through because at midnight, you can sing a break through into your life.

God Blesses at midnight.

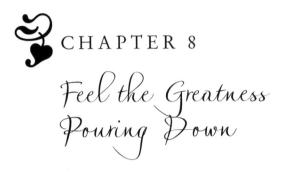

CHAPTER 8

Feel the Greatness Pouring Down

With closed eyes, this was given to me by the Holy Spirit.

Sitting in my chair one day, with my eyes closed not asleep, but in deep reminisce, the holy spirit said to me in a sweet loving voice.

Feel the greatness pouring down.

I immediately opened my eyes not in a haste, but at a gentle paste. I continue to caress the greatness the Lord was speaking about.

Contemplating on this greatness God mentioned, a greatness no man can give to you.

This greatness will definitely come from God, no unholy hands or un anointed hands would be able to touch this greatness.

It will be a consuming fire so strong, that if anyone came close to you, they will be consumed in the flames of the anointing that is given to me

This greatness will be so enormous, no one can withstand that level, and gravity of this anointed greatness. That level of power, will go beyond men knowledge.

The holy spirit said, this anointed greatness will be handed over to you like, the pouring down of a Mighty gush of water bursting out of the cloud.

He is pouring out of me a mighty promise that have not yet been seen even by the prophets of old, because they went on before.

This will be a continuation of their blessing, which is being handed over to me with lightening speed.

He said, continue this leg by the guidance of the Holy Spirit.

Even though this was given to, me it can also be used by hungry spirit that thrust after God vigorously.

If you are that person, take time to claim it for your life also in Jesus name. For this blessings from God is for all who desire that dimension of this anointing. Bask in his glorious presence, and holiness.

Quench that parch ness within you, that desires to be watered by the holy ghost fire.

Amen.

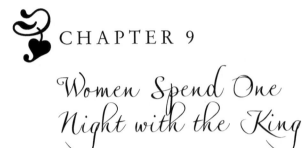

CHAPTER 9

Women Spend One Night with the King

Most times you underestimate yourselves women.

I can never understand why.

Could it be that there is a form of inferiority complex, that comes to steel your beliefs? I want to tell you right here and now, you are all beautiful royalty, who belongs to Elohim (One of Power). I am not just talking from the lips, you were exclusively created by a loving God, our Lord and savor Jesus Christ, who has class, and taste in anything he creates, and you know what?, you are one of them.

Never let anyone tell you different, stand, and take a few second looking inwardly, you will see every part is unique. Do not focus on your looks, size, knowledge, or accent. Keep your focus on God, and lay everything before him. Be excited of who you are, and use your mental strength to excel you to the dimension, the King of kings want you to go. Do not give anyone permission to stipulate, who you are. Ester did not meditate on her situation of being an orphan girl, who grew up in exile in Persia, who was brought up by her cousin Mordecai (Ester 2:5:7). She step into the open gates of the palace when time permit, with head held high. She eventually became, the beauty queen of Persia who received enormous favor from King Ahasuerus.

Could it be, as a little girl, she had photogenic memory of this palace, as she pass by on many occasions, never thinking, that one day she will enter as a proprietor. That is totally God. You can now do the same precious women of God.

Visualize yourself in a palace, and you are familiar with a real king, isn't it true, you will have total access of a real queen?

Why wait to enter a palace to feel this way, you are who you make yourself to be, beauty is inward, and outward. Stand and look into your mirror, you will see a reflection of the only one who can hinder herself.

Until you believe, and allow yourself to visualize you being in the king palace, even if its just for one night you will see how important you are to the rose of Sharon, and to yourself. By then you will start walking on the queenly path towards beauty, the way God meant it to be for you, from the very day you were created.

Don't be afraid to make yourself beautiful, you might ask, how can I do this?

Let me tell you, we know God give man knowledge to invent and create beauty lines, but the best beauty package you can purchase, is being in the company of the King himself, and letting yourself loose, and free in the ushering of his presence into your life.

There and then you will see, the woman you were created to be.

Come forth woman. Let the dew (grace) wet you totally, as you glide into position.

The woman that was hidden deep within you yourself did not know she was there.

Smile in the mirror to yourself with an introductory mode and repeat this.

Hi!

Please to meet you _____, say your name, and tell yourself.

This is the Kings daughter, speaking to you from inside the palace itself. Stay in the palace, because its your new place of residence. Set your shoes inside the doorway, push open the windows, allowing the fresh air of the green mountains to blow through, as you bask in the knowledge of your permanent residence.

Claim it now, choose the area in the palace you prefers best.

Maybe its in the living room, kitchen, den, or the court yard. Where ever you place yourself, is where you will be.

I will choose the official living room, that is where you will be able to perform in royalty, with exceptional attitude like the kings daughter. Allow your mind to trace the compound, that you now own, its your inheritance that was willed to you, by the king himself Jesus Christ. Accept your gift as of being the king daughter. Keeping in mind royalty runs through your veins, from your Master, Jesus Christ.

CHAPTER 10

Be a Worshiping Woman of God Like Lydia (Acts 16-14)

If you can only be as desirous like the woman of Thyatira in Acts-16-11.

She was Lydia a merchant woman of expensive purple cloth, and other than being a woman of class, she was also a worshiper of God.

She sat and listen to the missionary. As she listen the Lord opened her heart, and she accepted what Paul was saying, she then got baptized, she could save her whole household, and lead them to the Lord.

Everyone in her household were saved.

She became faithful to the Lord, that she invited the disciples as her guest.

Lydia told them, if you agree I am faithful to the Lord, come stay at my home, she urges, them and they stayed.

As women we must strive in a desperate mood to be a woman fromThyatiria. Lydia press through into the teaching of the disciples, because she was famished and thirsty for what they had, she was also able to save her whole household, and lead them the Lord.

We could question ourselves at times asking, why was she able to capture her whole household. We can say the soil of life is fertile, what ever you sow will grow and bring forth fruit, good or bad. In this case Lydia sow good and it paid a visit to her home.

I also believe their was a shifting through her in a way that could never have gone un noticed. This had to be a great outpouring of anointing from the Holy Spirit.

The holy spirit is challenging you now, to prove to him you are a woman of God who can even be more effective to your family than Lydia was.

If you retrace the history of the Bible, you will notice their were some great prophets. Imagine if you can obtain this great power, I must say even greater power from God what mighty warriors you will be.

In order for us to obtain this, we must stand on the word, and stay in the word of the great I am.

Their must be a mood within us for a vicious desire of holiness. It has to be like the women of old, who did not compromise the word of God no matter what came their way, they were known as true worshipers.

We recalled, Lydia listen to the disciples when God opened her heart.

Lets learn to listen. We must pray for open ears, and hungry hearts, and edifying of the holy word of God.

We recall she said to the disciples, if you agree that I am faithful, come stay at my home, and they did stay.

Guess why?

They knew by the direction of the Holy Spirit she was honestly faithful, she did not just speak the word faithfully she lived it, and this allowed the light to shine through.

Let us shine a light, that no natural eyes can behold, unless they get into a convicted realm of God. Invite the fire of the holy spirit, to reside within you. Remove the old wine skin, and replace it with new wine that has never been touched. Activate that anointing God has given you by praying, fasting and feeding in the word of God daily. Falling prostrate (Laying Flat) at Jesus feet.

I want you to make a promise with God, to be joint airs with Jesus, ask him to break, and mold you over into a new person, totally equip to deal with the new era of hurting and needy people of the world.

It has to be all for the glory of God no less.

Amen.

CHAPTER 11

And She Girded Her Loins

At the Genesis of times, when Eve were deceived in the garden of Eden, we read all about the punishment that occur upon her, which was automatically transferred to all women from that day on.

The punishment was, that all women will bear children in the most gruesome of pain.

We may say, what the enemy meant for bad God turned it around for the good.

You might be wondering, why do we have to endure such pressure. I guess the grapes ask the wine that same question. Selah.

As women, you are known to be the weakest vessel in the Bible, and the word of God say we should be treated as such, we will not argue about that because we are. That weakness is based on our gentle dimina and unique tendency, that surrounds us.

When it comes to child bearing, we are super charged and energized.

God gave us the strength to be able to stand the gruesome pain of giving birth, and from their on, women use that strength in their household, as a mother to her kids and wife to her husband.

When it comes to her family the weight of everyday hustle is never to heavy.

She gird herself up, and prepare for what each day has to offer. You should give yourself a round of applause women. They might drive you insane at times, but in their mind and heart they could never have done this without you. This is how important, the strength you holds within is

Don't throw in the towel, but gird up yourself with the true and living word. Their lies the strength of the lion that roars within.

CHAPTER 12

The Tag Team— Deborah and Jael

From one woman to the other.

Now Deborah was the name of the New Testament woman.

The name of Deborah means Honey Bee, Psalm 118:12 & Isaiah 7:18.

The first Deborah was Rebecca's nurse Gen-35:8.

She died on their way to Bethel, with her master Jacob's household, and she was buried at Alton Bacuth which means the Oak of Weeping.

This indicated, she was much loved, and was a long time companion of Rebecca. The second Deborah however was unique, she was a prophetess and judge.

Her position as a prophetess, showed her messages was from God.

That was not unique in the bible, but was unusual. Deborah herself was unique, she was the only woman ever to judge Israel before major events, that marks her story.

Her husband was Lapidate, he went unknown in the bible. Deborah was known as the mother of Israel.

Now Deborah who judge Israel did her duties from the office under a Palm tree between Ramah, and Bethel in Mt Ephraim, and the children of Israel came to her for judgment.

One day she sent to call Barak, son of Abinoam of Kedesh in

Naphtal and said unto him, didn't God command you to go to Mt Tabor?, taking ten thousand men, and children of Zebuimn to the river Kishon.

And Sisera, the captain of Jabin's army with his Chariots, and his multitude and I will deliver him unto thine hand?

Then Barak told Deborah, I will go only if you go with me. She said very well, I will go with you, but their will be consequences since you made that choice.

You will receive no honor, and the Lord victory over Sisera will be handed into the hands of a woman.

He agreed, and Deborah led the army, as she marched with them to Sisera.

They got the news, that Barak had gone to Mt Tabor, he gathered nine hundred of his iron chariots, and all his warriors, and they marched to the Kishon River.

Deborah then said to Barak, get ready, today the Lord will give you victory over Sisera because, the Lord is marching ahead in our Army. Halal Praise in Heaven,

The Lord then threw Sisera, and his charioteers and warriors into panic, "Ha". Sisera then jump of his chariot and escaped on foot, little did he know, it was a tag team taking place between Deborah and Jael.

Go Girls!!

Deborah and Barak had no worry after, and you will here why later on. They concentrated on completing the mission, and that they did.

Not one of Sisera nine hundred men was standing, they all fell upon the edge of their swords, Sisera then abandoned his Army.

Now Herber a Kenite Moses son-in-law, had move away from members of his tribe, and pitch a tent with his wife Jael by the oak of Zanannim near Kedish.

There is where Sisera headed, direct to the tent, and it so happen Deborah partner was at home in her tent waiting for her husband Herber return, instead she had to greet their enemy.

But she did not show a evil heart.

Jael was as gentle as a lamb, Sisera ask her for a drink of water, but she gave him a strong glass of milk. He then told her to keep watch, be careful who keep watch at your door.

Sisera told Jael if anyone ask for me, tell them you did not see me

She then covered him and waited to here him let out the tired snore, and she crept up to him with a tent peg, and she drove it through his temple into the ground, and he died.

Barak came soon after, and Jael told him come and see the man you are looking for, he is dead in the tent.

The winner was the tag team girls Deborah and Jael. From that day on Israel became stronger. Jael became blessed above all women in tents, because of her help to the Lord.

Sisera ask for water, but she gave him milk in a bowl fit for a King.

That was the last we heard of Deborah. Gideon became the next judge of Israel.

You can do all things through Christ who strengthen you (Philippians: 4: 13).

Who would imagine God will use a woman to lead an army, he is no respecter of persons, as long as you make yourselves available, you shall have the victory in any thing you touch, and agree upon, as long as God is leading.

March on with the holy ghost fire upon your feet women, and be sure you pick a good team player, if not you can leave the axe handle outside, to return as a nightmare (2 Kings-6), but if you get rid of it totally you will benefit greatly. Not only you in the future will be blessed, but your generations who will come after you.

Tag team with positive and alert people, and the conquest will be yours. Watch your inner circle closely. You run from Deborah, and you ended up within Jael tent, the perfect catch of the day.

CHAPTER 13

After the Shipwreck

Paul could have entered into a disappointed, and a don't want to continue attitude, as some persons might have done.

But he did not.

He used that time of the shipwreck to be positive, he took great and enormous advantage of that time in Malta where he could witness, and minister to the spiritually illiterate.(Act:27). Paul could have sat around pondering and focusing on the evil ones who were seeking to devour him.

He operated in a carefree attitude, focusing on winning the lost at any cost with a passion.

No matter what was being thrown at him, he kept on seeking to use the disappointment for the fulfillment of the work he had on his schedule, which must be completed without delay, because time was running out for Paul.

We must realize in a speedy time to keep focus no matter what is being thrown your way.

Lets learn to use it as a stepping stone towards winning the prize. I really admire Paul in the book of Acts, and would take certain patterns after him, he made me realize that no matter how horrendous the ship wreck we might face is. At some point and time in life, you don't have to stay their.

It teaches us to swim a little way after the wreck, hold your head above water, and stroke the waves with determination and humbleness, consistency, strength, and while you stroke let your mind be thinking what is the next move God will want you to do.

And when you stand on the land after the ship wreck, don't look back keep walking with your head held high, and greet the new strange land as though nothing was wrong, because in the sprit nothing is wrong, that is just a point where God is allowing you to rest before moving on to the other Dimension.

Always remember a ship wreck is not a miss hap. it's a step to the other level, for the call of duties assigned to you. Use your disappointments and mishap as your stepping stone.

Move On. Begin your walk up the larder of God promises for you.

CHAPTER 14

Women of Expensive Perfume

As you might know, the fragrance of an expensive high quality perfume carries an aroma that not even by doing the laundry, with the best detergent can it be removed.

That's the sign, and proof it's a top of the line perfume.

What happens when you wear this fragrance is, where ever you passes or enter your presence, and attention will at all times capture the seeing or viewing audience

Sometimes remarks will be made towards you the individual, or visual contact will be obvious.

You might ask your self questions at times, and the answer will be simple, the quality of fragrance first of all will differentiate your category from other's due to the value of that perfume, not everyone will be able to afford that brand.

The other thing is, a special light has shone through, that is why you have captured an audience.

This is my point, as women, God should at all times, where ever you go, who ever you speak to, what ever company you are in, what ever you do be sure to allow your lives to be an example of fragrance.

You should be like valuable perfume, that when ever you pass through a place, that fragrance would remain in minds and taught, and the remarks will be indeed, this is really really a woman of God. Their should be such an expensive rich fragrance of Holiness Virtuousness reflecting through you as you worship the Holy Spirit filled with a special glow coming through hungering for God, with great desperation.

That is where other's will start searching themselves, while yearning with jealousy for this fragrance you carry around with you, the Holy Spirit.

If you recall in the book of Ester (Ester 2-12) before the king could meet, and see queen Ester she had to soak in Myre and Frankincense, and perfume of high quality before she could enter. And when she did enter the room where the King would be awaiting her presence, he would always be in amaze and Orr of Queen Ester because she was viewed way above what he has ever seen.

This is a level where we should covet to reach in Christ Jesus.

Women, you should never settle for mediocre, or less than the plan God has for you. Let our desire thirst for growing stronger and stronger every day.

You will receive great fragrance according to your desire and passion.

The more you submerge in to the word, the more fragrance will capture the nostrils of God, the more you desire to sop with the holy spirit, the more your fragrance will affect others.

Stretch forth, and reach high up to the one that holds the expensive fragrance, his name is Jesus Christ, and let him know you are interested, and desperate with un- limited anxiety, in purchasing a top of the line high fragrance perfume, let him know your urgency and he will do the rest.

Be sure you have what it takes to purchase that line, because it is not cheap.

The price you might have to pay before you receive this fragrance is, humility, patience, sealed Lips, peace, forgiveness, tolerance, love and more.

How bad do you want to be a Fragrance of light, and a Fragrance of high quality within?

CHAPTER 15

Your Immaturity Can Delay Your Blessings

Did this ever cross your mind, you have been praying for a long time, grinding your knees on the floor, using up roll of paper towel along with bath towels, weeping to God and petitioning him with all the please in the book you could think about, and still there is no answer from the grate high priest, who owns everything under heaven and earth.

Have you ever really wonder why is this? Its called immaturity. This can happen if you are outside the will of God, and this can hinder his plans for you. God is in control of us, he is your father who is like parents who knows their children. The word knowing is a powerful word (Full Awareness). I use this word because God knows us, even more than we know ourselves. He knew us even while we were in our mothers womb. God will be able to detect, and know if we are capable to handle what you are asking for at that present time, and like a parent he knows without a shadow of a doubt, if you are ready to handle an adult task. This is how God determines if you are ready, if you are mature enough to handle what we are asking for.

My recommendation to you is this, do not fight the delay, that would be wasted time. If you do it will be like a drowning man in the ocean, the more he fights the more dangerous, and difficult it becomes for him to be saved from the predicament he is in.

All you have to do is seek God and retrieve studies and teachings in maturity. This is where, the bath towel and paper towel comes in.

Cry out to God and make yourself available to walk in mature ness

When you submit to hungering and thirst for more of God, you will eventually be come a mature person in Christ.

I assure you this, you will realize, and recognize what was hindering your blessing from coming a long time ago, just a word with so little letters that has such big meaning, so big that it can hinder your whole well being of life

Immaturity.

When your kids are not mature enough we keep them in a waiting area until we see they are ready.

That is what God does to you.

The longer you are disobedient, the longer the wait will be, and we all know that no one ever likes to wait. We need every thing in a microwave time. I tell you today you can be in all the rush in the world. Unless you are not mature enough, you will be your own set back for what ever you are raining down all those tears for.

No one can do this for you, you got to do this for yourself, you got to be willing.

First you must remain humble, it might be the hardest thing to do, but it will be worth it all at the end.

The only way humility comes is when you show how bad you desire your blessings, and how soon you want it to arrive.

If you do not humble yourself you are going against the word of God.

He that humblest himself or herself shall be exulted, and I am sure I read that in the Bible, Matthew - 23:12. I am positive you did also.

BELIEVE!!

You might miss it deliberately or skip over the word humble. I want to say to you now, your delay is up to you.

Maturity is knocking at your door, will you answer? God bless.

CHAPTER 16

Let's Dine with John as He Speaks to the Ladies

Reading from 2nd John i realize he was speaking in this letter specially to the lady, and her children. He used a remark like this.

Who I love in the truth, as does everyone else who knows the truth of God.

He then bless the livers of truth by saying, may Grace, Mercy and Peace which comes from God our father, and from Jesus Christ be with you who live in truth.

We can see the importance of living in truth, there is great benefits within laying up for, us who always stay in the truth.

It was an Orr moment for, me when I read where he was reminding us to love one another. Why was John specifically speaking to Ladies.

I would like to back track a bit to wives and the word submit. Submitting in any form is humbling, with a loving personality.

We can see there is a built in emotion, that should be natural and truthful within us. (Love is a verb) John said love is doing what God commanded us to do.

He reminded us to watch out for those who will try to divert you from loving each other, that includes the adversary, they are in disbelief of God.

Be alert!Such persons are like the antichrist.

Be vigilant, do not loose the prize for which we have been working so hard towards, be diligent so you will receive your full reward. John ask that we continue in the teaching of God. He was really serious about this, because he said further on, don't continue a relationship with someone who does not teach the truth of God, and do not invite him into your home, because you do not want to encourage him in anyway in believing his immature knowledge is appreciated. (Luke -18-1-8)The word of God teaches, if anyone encourages him they becomes a partner of his evil works. So you see, there is no change in our own mentality, and what you think, but its all about how God told us to live and what to do.

We learn from John to be honest, and truthful in all we do think and speak. While keeping in mind submission comes with two kind of love.

Heavenly Love which is a selfless, and unconditional love with compassion accompanied, and Earthly Love is a love which is based only on what you can receive. I say choose wisely, because it comes back to you in full measures. Let our words be seasoned with salt (Colossians 4-6)

Always remember, it is all for the Lord and savior Jesus Christ.

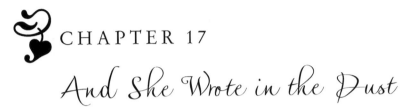

CHAPTER 17

And She Wrote in the Dust

You have the ability to free yourself from your past with power, and authority from the Lord Jesus Christ, and it is imperative to do so. He is flammable, and can destroy any shame or disgrace that may have invaded your space, while keeping you in bondage. That's a scheme from the enemy.

As Jesus was speaking one morning the teacher of religious law, and Pharisees brought a woman they caught in the act of adultery.

They put her in front of the crowd saying teacher.

This woman was caught in the very act of adultery, and the law of Moses say to stone her, what do you say?

But Jesus stooped. Stooping in my opinion is a position of authority, and strength, hallelujah to Jesus. (John-8:8)

We all heard Jesus stooped, and wrote in the dust, we never really knew what he wrote, all we know he wrote.

Maybe we can say he wrote, he who is without sin cast the first stone.

According to what we read, he could have stayed in the stooping position to speak, and stood up to answer the crowd.

Never the less, their were definitely some note taking in the dust.

Maybe the notes was forgive, and you shall be forgiven

Is it possible Jesus wrote, they are all God children? Is it possible he said as in Proverb 11-, a fool is quick tempered, but a wise person remains calm when insulted. He might have wrote, those who judge shall be judge, Is it possible that he wrote their will be a shifting, those who are in the front will go to the back, and those at the back shall be brought to the front. Is it possible he wrote, those who are in premature high places shall come down and those who are fully matured shall rise up, I can proceed.

What ever he wrote, it spoke for each and every one of the human race. From the oldest to the youngest disappeared one after the next.

Jesus said to the woman who was never named, and who were left standing alone, where are your accusers?

Did not even one of them condemn you?

She said in a thankful voice, No Lord.

Jesus said Neither do I.

Go and sin no more my daughter. God forgives from the greatest to the least of sins. He throws your sins into the sea of forgetfulness. Never condemn others who are less fortunate, and weak in controlling their own brain, and body when the time arrive to do so.

Help them by using the word of God, and not judge them, always keeping in mind Judge and you will be judged. (Matthew 7:1)

Be alert in hearing, while deleting the voices of the wicked, and listen to the voice of the most high God and Savior Jesus Christ.

Go, and sin no more, God have forgiven you. Maybe you feel bared in like there is no hope, and no way of exit, thinking your sins are at depths that is unreachable. I say no, God hands is extendable to reach you where ever you may be, never allowing criticism to put a veil over your head. Daughters of the most high know this, failure is a stair way to success. Where you started is not where you are going to finish. Never bow your head down in shame. and if you do bow your head, let it be to look at your feet, that will escort you to a higher place in Christ. you are not women of fear. You are not a woman of fear, you are women of faith, activate it. Stretch your hands forth, he will take it and eject you out of your circumstances. Here is where you shout hallelujah.

CHAPTER 18

Dreams Do Come Through

A question for you.

How big is your dreams?

How bad do you want it?

You see God do make dreams come through, but you must be desperate for it, you must be willing to chase after it, and you must be ready to wrestle all night if it takes that long, as long as you show God your meaningful desperate passion for him, he will do the rest.

<u>It's all up to you</u>

The door is open for you to walk into your ministry, your anointing, your blessing, and your destiny. You have untouched potential.

Prize out of your comfort zone, and get into position, allowing boldness to be your cloak and the blood of Jesus your leader.

<u>Do you know who you are?</u>

You are the king's children, start walking into the throne room he has prepared for you.

Dreams do become reality ladies.

Big dreams plus purpose equals destiny.

Big for your family, big for your position at your work place, big for your spiritual life.

Joseph had a dream, and we all know where, and how it started, and how it ended.

With your dream comes jealousy, watch out for that, then comes throwing him into a pit.

Sometimes you have to lay in the pit, just for a short time before you step out, so don't get to comfortable their.

He was then sold, you may have to be sold out to Jesus, then imprisoned in quietness, all for a short time allowing purpose to lead.

It will give you time to stop, and focus on the mighty King of Kings. Always remember God will use your own pharaoh to get you into the palace. He will remove a Vashti to create space for the queen Ester within you, but with all of this you must be prepared to go through, because dream do birth into reality.

I am excited because I know, the master is getting ready to birth power within you all as women of God. Power to face the world, power to be mentors, power to be better in your marriages, power to be women of great examples, power to be excellent in all God is directing you to be.

Grab a hold now and receive what the redeemer Lord and savior Jesus Christ, has in store for you. Learn to stand on the covenant of the word women, as you equip yourself with the heavy artilleries the bible.

In blessing he will bless you, in multiplying he will multiply thy seed as the stars of the heavens.

Genesis 22:17 claims his promise today is for you, and your life will take a 360 degree turn towards excellence in Christ Jesus, which will eventually change your life forever. Women rise up to your call, and do what you were designed to do.

Position yourself to hook up to a spiritual Dialysis, removing the old, and taking in the new.

This is an order from God.

This could be your season ladies for change.

Come out from your comfort zone, and identify your gifts, and run with it.

If you do not use it, you will loose it, its your time to hit center stage for kingdom building.

God is getting ready to use women like never before.

Would you be left behind?

Would you become a God leading Lady?

If you recall the first person who saw Jesus when he was resurrected, was a woman, (Mary Magdalene).

The first person to lead an Army, was a woman (Deborah the prophetess (Judges:4), and the first person to be a judge was a woman. Exodus from your comfort zone precious women of God and rise up.

Be mindful, there was a first in everyone who came before you.

It is up to you.

Do like Johasephat in (2 Chronicles 20:21) and pray, being confident God mercy endures forever, that's your confidence.

Stand up, and step out with possessiveness ladies, and take a bow. Its your time. Dreams do come through.

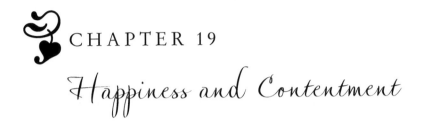

CHAPTER 19

Happiness and Contentment

While interacting with my husband one morning about people, and what it takes to make them achieve happiness, we realized the answer was nothing under heaven, and earth.

They can have a multitude of wealth, from billions to trillions of dollars, mansions on a hill, portraying to the universe they are the happiest human beings on earth.

We figure out that some are living a gigantic lie. Really and truly they are exploding on the inside, they have no peace, no love, no joy, and no happiness. My husband said to me through his anointed lips. The only way you can judge a man happiness, is through peace, joy and contentment. I was listening to here him unfold this unique description, of the fake happy faces walking around.

He said to me their is different levels in life.

Extremely rich, rich, poor, which is the less fortunate, and extremely poor.

I heard this description from my husband in 2008, and I was amazed, at the same time not amaze of what came out of his anointed lips, but amaze to see the picture in this light, and what God is doing. I see a powerful modern day Elijah, who speaks with authority, and fearlessness, while delivering to who ever he is led to. When i heard him repeat this revelation on January 6th 2010 at 7:28 am, after our devotion, it ignite something within me again, that was so true. I want to say as an echo of my husband, things in and on this earth cannot bring peace, joy nor happiness. He said to me, people fight to achieve stuff in life, they want the biggest house, and when they acquire it they are happy for the first month, then their they go again being un happy, they then set out to acquire a new car, clothes, shoes, the works, thinking these things will bring them happiness, then they realize there is no peace, and happiness in things.

Things are for a second, but peace, joy, happiness and contentment is for a life time.

He went on to elaborate a little more, on what he meant when he said about their level of contentment, he said a person will have a donkey, and one will have the most expensive car, and we may look at the one with the donkey's condition, and feel pity for him, but little do we know, the person at that level is enormously happier than the man with the expensive vehicle.

You see, at that lower level that person is familiar with that life style, and in his world he is happy, and has very little bills to meet, we can say very little headache. Where as the rich man has a multitude of things to keep up with, such as huge bills, maintenance of the mansion security and so much more trying to keep up a façade (appearance)

He has to maintain this rich stature, where as the man with the donkey have very little people to impress, all he need is the basic necessities and he will be alright.

This is what you call being content, and happy at your level. You may look, and feel pity for him who have little, but who you should really be sorry for is the man with the expensive car. The more he has, the more unhappy he remains and the one with the donkey and very little remains happy because that's his level of contentment. Happiness don't stare at what people acquire and speak about, it's the understanding that they are happy in their own level of content.

There is no joy without the Lord Jesus Christ in your life, when you have God in your vessels, their will be happiness, joy and contentment, not in the things of this world but within your body and soul. When you have God in your vessel, you can smile at the storm. Keep in mind, the only way you can judge a man, is by the happiness, joy and contentment in their heart.

Relationship Revelation

In the midst of your joy, think about your sorrow.

In the midst of your sorrow, think about your joy.

You have God to serve, a part to walk, a journey to take, and a life to live.

A relationship is like building a house that will never be completed, but you have to keep on building, its like a leaky ship on the sea, you have to keep bailing out the water to stay a float.

If you stop you will sink, its like breathing while we keep inhaling, and exhaling.

Yes. If you stop you will die, and so will your relationship.

So keep on breathing, and keep working on your relationship. Remember a relationship is a ship with the two persons in it, if you want a good and successful journey, let the Lord be your captain.

We all are sheep, let the Lord be our Sheppard.

CHAPTER 20

Who am I?

It's a question you should cease at times, look directly into a mirror, and ask yourselves who am i?

When you ask that question you will really see what a wonderful woman of importance, and excellence you are.

You are a woman of purpose, a woman of beauty, a woman of faith, a woman of quality and a daughter of the most high king. I am sure you did not know this, I am positive you never took the time out to really love yourself. Maybe you never took the time out to tell God thanks for making you in this unique way, in his image and likeness.

You take time to look out for everyone else, you take the time to care for everyone else making sure everything is so perfect and in order, and never took time with you personally.

Come on women of purpose, God word told us, in order to love others you first must love yourselves, and when you find that love In your heart for yourselves, then people, family, and friends will all become naturally lovable to you.

In order to achieve this personality, you must begin to build a towering self esteem, with head held high, always maintaining humility. Questions might be asked, how will I do this? First you must believe in yourself, believe you are beautiful in looks, shape, knowledge. Believe who God say you are. You are who you believe you are. It is imperative you believe this positively without any waver in mind. You must build a bold and graceful tone of speech, that way you will not be fearful to speak any where, or be between any great crowd. Its your prerogative.

Be prepared for where God is taking you. Build up an attitude that blocks out negative words that might be thrown upon you at times, that is a trick of the devil to degrade and be little you.

You will soon find out, no matter what you do it may not be appreciated no matter what you do, you may not be praised by man.

When you see this, don't be afraid, and do not feel dis-hearted.

Praises from man is just tempory, and for a short term, sometimes its design to make you feel good.

I urge you to look for your praise from God, that is the one who will never lead you wrong, and who will always give you the praise of assurance for a job well done.

Looking to man for credit at times can put a cloud over your spirit.

Without Christ in your vessel, you can be hurt, feeling depreciated, and like a reject, that is why you need to do your best at all times and keep your eyes on Jesus.

Don't ever look left nor right, start disciplining yourself to build a wall, that blocks out the sound of certain remarks. It must be a wall which can be like a car window, that rolls up and down when the negative, and be littleing words are thrown upon you, when its words of honest praise you wind it down, and when it's the wall of negativity you wind, up so you will build a barrier to only here positive words speaking into your life, that way you will start elevating yourself in Christ to be mature and a better women, wives, mothers, who are great in all you do. always remember to remind yourself of who you are. If it so happens that some negative words were slip through the crack, always remember to remind yourself of who you are.

Remember, you are a woman God has created uniquely.

When you get to that level, you will believe and realize this strongly, nothing else will distract, or hinder your path to spiritual prosperity then you will know you are heading towards perfection in strength, to cope with the everyday trials life sometimes offer to you. Keep your eyes at all times on Jesus ladies, if he watches over the sparrow, just know he definitely watches over you, and when you know you have a shield around you, their will be no fear of what man say or do. Take a walk to the mirror in private, with no one else in your room, look into that mirror face to face, and ask yourself this question.

Who am I?

Stand there and don't move, keep steering until you receive an answer, and believe me you will.

At that point, you will be changed into the woman God created you to be, the woman who was hiding in that package for so long. Their will be a blinding light that take position in your mirror.

Come on ladies. Slam open that door, kick that concrete wall down, and come on out. Breath, the writing you will see in your mirror will read, I am a winner, I am un shakable in Christ, I am beautiful, I am unique, and I have total confidence, there is hidden power within you (me).

I have total confidence there is hidden power within.

CHAPTER 21
The Showcase God

I really need a car a house, and lots of money, while you are it God, can you get me a speed boat, and remember to throw in the Anointing, don't hold back give it to me in full measure. I don't want to be rude God but can you put a rush on the blessings?

I need to get to an appointment soon.

And opps! I forget to tell you, I cannot attend bible study on Friday, also church on Sunday is a no, because my friends are going to a picnic, and I can't let them down, being there is a must.

Well! I am true with you God, now let me head to the show case, and put you back, maybe I should dust him first, and keep him safe in the case for easy access.

Hmm, where should I put the key?

Maybe I will leave it in the draw next to the case, where it can be retrieved quick. It may seem amusing and funny now as you read, but it is extremely serious what some people does, and it is also a shame. The supreme sovereign mighty, none like him God, who we are to worship praise and give our all to are treated this way. Having God as your convenience, and an ornament when in times of need is preposterous.

Did you ever imagine what it would be like if God were to treat us this way?

Come on lets be realistic, and I need you to ponder on this.

If every time we need something from God he say ok Gabriel, check and see if there is any space in the showcase, if there is, put this person in and lock it

until I am ready get him or her out, as a matter fact I think I will leave them there for about forty years no matter if they kept knocking, or shouting do not let them out. Leave them there until I need them to do a work for me, or when I am ready to use them. That is how you treat God.

He is there ready and waiting to meet your needs, show you love, give you high favor, bless you in abundance, spiritually, financially, physically and other wise.

Come on, we need to appreciate God to the fullest and not when you are in need, you head over to the show case in a hurry, and when you are finish place him back. This is an extremely sorry state.

Did you ever take note, when you ask God for anything no matter what, if the time span of your request is speedy or in a delay mode. If this is so, start searching yourself and the way in which you approach the master.

God word gave us the authority to ask, it is our right to approach him at any time of needs, by the theology dictionary of laws, we are in order when we ask. The veil was torn to permit us that access

No where in the Bible say it must happen in a rush, and it have to be only when we need stuff desperately, take God out from the show case.

I am positive you never read that.

The word say and this is in a decisive way, not a negative with humility, ask and it shall be given, knock and will be open, seek and you shall find, and never in a rush.

God is not an employee of any carrier service, he is the God who owns the universe, and will take care of his children. He will never let the righteous be forsaken nor his seed begging for bread (Psalm 37:25), he also said in the word, he will never leave us nor forsake us. (Deuteronomy 31:8) Why not stand on his word today, why not take God out of that dusty show case, and as a matter fact destroy that whole case, just incase you are tempted to use it again, there will be no case there and you will have no choice but to keep him in your heart and mind at all times where he belongs, recognizing and realizing there is none like him and none to compare to God. I urge you to take God at his word because.

He is not a show case God. He is the awesome wonder of the universe.

CHAPTER 22

Never Listen to a Naughty Tongue

It is a wonderful thing to remain level headed, and not be easily side tracked, as the enemy will taunt you to do.

Our God the mighty King of Kings Elohim Yashuah has created you to be ambassador to represent the king and kingdom, and as some already realize God has a course charted out for each individuals, each and every one of you are in line for your schedule task, believe me, the devil knows just that and will be on your every move to prevent this from materializing.

I say no!

Never ever allow this distraction. Apply the blood of Jesus.

How will you know which way to handle this situation. First of all you need to build a block here. Start building by using the word of God as often as it takes, and never listen to negative talk, gossip, here say, idle talks, this is a trap the enemy uses to side track you into shifting from the mark God has upon you.

When situation come with agitation accompanying, just know this, one of the problem he uses, is to pull you of the road God has chartered for you.

If we notice Job never ever allowed any of those situations to pause him, or cause him to look left nor right, and that is a great pattern we should crave to adapt. He kept his eyes on the Christ Jesus who at all times was looking over him.

His friends came with naughty tongues, but Job kept looking to the master. Even his wife said to him why not curse God and die (Job 2:9).

His words to her were, oh foolish woman and he never allowed any negative or naughty tongue to shift his attention.

I say this to you my queens be careful, of what and who you listen to.

Reserve your ears only for the feeding of spiritual edification from the Holy Spirit.

Time is to important to waste listening to naughty words which cannot mature your spiritual life. We are in a season of urgency, for the signs of the time is in close visual view.

Try your best to start delegating things that are of no benefit to your future in your walk with Jesus Christ.

It's a trap.

Do not be wheeled in by the enemy web. Stay rooted and grounded in the word of Jesus Christ your Redeemer.

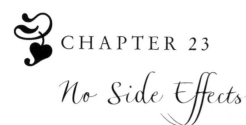

CHAPTER 23

No Side Effects

Taking a view at the goodness of God, our Savior and Lord with confidence, and what an awesome wonder he is, capture the taught, of how people who when problems arrive their place of refuge most times is, the drug house, witch doctor, voodoo man, and physic. They run every where else, a friend and strangers, but hardly go to God. The God we serve is Jehovah Jeirah the great provider, Jehovah rapha the mighty healer, Jehovah Sharma, he is always there, Jehovah shalom, the peace maker, Jehovah tsidkenu, who is righteous. He teaches us nothing is to difficult for him to handle. You got permission from God when he told us to ask, and it will be given, knock and it shall be open. The great physician, no doctor can do what God can. He gives them the knowledge to do what they do, but still they can make mistakes that will never be made by God. God has the remedy for anything, circumstances, situation, and with his remedy comes no side effect. When people run for quick fixes to rectify conditions, it comes with a package like illuminations, sickness, death, jail time, and all these are no good, but with God, our Lord and savior Jesus Christ, the blood comes with power, victory, peace, the anointing. And what is so awesome about this is, they are all organic with no side effects.

My adorable sisters I pray, that you trust Jesus Christ always, and get high on the holy spirit and fire.

You will prove and endorse, that serving God has no side effects.

God is the peace maker and the miracle worker, who is marvelous, great and wonderful. I invite you to come taste and see God is good. Remember he never will leave you, nor forsake you. Trust God, and give him your life totally today. I pray the holy spirit will arrest your heart, and soul, with extreme conviction, that will eventually. lead you to follow Christ, through water baptism. in Jesus, mighty name.

Repeat This Pray.
God wonder of the universe
Who hold no grudge against me, (you)
Who holds no hate towards me
I ask you to come into my life
Accept me just as I am
Blemishes and all
Deliver me from the snare of the fowler
Take me out of the enemy grasp
And into your care
Cover me under your wings
And deliver me from my sins, known, and un known in Jesus name.
I accept the invitation God
To be apart of the family of God
I count it a privilege to sit in your presence
And I pray all this in no other name but your name, Lord and savior Jesus Christ. Amen.

CHAPTER 24

It Shows in Your Worship

Worship is a feeling of expression of reverence and adoration Where we honor and todah, with open hands. as our eternal rock of ages ignites that flame within, that causes your worship to be glamorously foolish before God With extravagant love and extreme submission to him. Caressing God with admiration for devotion where we barauch, get on our knees. It is so beautiful my women of God. Your action will show how much you believe in Jesus Christ.

When you act carefree in your pray and worship, that is showing your denial in God and his awesomeness.

When you give your all in worshiping the Lion of Judah, it shows you believe there is a God, and his name is Jesus Christ, who is deserving of our Todah without apologies, shame, and caring less of who may be looking at you. we are in a time and season where we must exercise selfishness towards man, while keeping focus only between you the individual and God.

There are times where we slope into the Thomas season, allowing doubt to take center stage. This portrays a fear which allows you to hide behind a screen, holding back on giving Elohim what he deserves. Thomas was told by the apostle Jesus is alive, he has risen, but he refuse to admit its true. He needed proof, he said, I must see the nail prints - John 20: 24:29.

This comes from lack of belief, faith, with doubt accompanying. You can show doubt through your pray and worship, while strolling in the Thomas mode. Needing desperately to see the pierce at his side before you believe.

Jesus could have ignored us on earth also, but he cared so much for his children, that he gave his life for you and I. Undeserving of his favor, he still sacrificed his only begotten son to save us. What wonderful blessings and privilege.

God has so much faith in his people, and always will. Do not rob him of his worship, he deserves ever second of it. He did not hold back on us, and that's a privilege to be appreciated to the full capacity.

Let it show in your worship. Replace shame, shyness and who might be looking, and worship God.

Let the mascara roll down your cheeks, let that wig fall of your head, let the white in your eyes turn red with tears. Jump, shout, dance, occupy the altar when the holy spirit push you, where ever and how ever the holy spirit arrest you my women of God., let it flow.

Allowing the warrior within you to rise like yeast in a dough, in Jesus Mighty name. How much do you believe in Jesus Christ, Yahweh Bore, the Lord our creator? Amen.

CHAPTER 25

The Our Father Pray Sermon

Pray was meant to be for the edification of our Spirit to exalt the Lord, and savior Jesus Christ, the son of God.

Pray is a solemn request or expression of thanks, and faith in the outcome. Pray is also a way of a communication process, that allows us to talk to God.

And also as a form of being personal with the master God.

Most time we run ahead of ourselves, and turn it into a show of who can pray the best and the longest, the our father pray was never meant to be a pray show case. as we learn in the book of (Matthew 6:5).

Jesus was speaking to the people teaching them about Pray and Fasting.

He specifically told them, when we pray publicity on street corners, and in the synagogues where everyone can see them that is the only reward they will ever receive, what a pitiful waste my people.

Jesus specifically said, when you pray to our father go by yourself, shut the door behind you and pray secretly and listen to this part. Only then, your father who knows all secrets not might reward you.

He said I will reward you.

I don't think we need to know more about the closet Pray,

He went on to say, when we pray do not babble on and on as people of other religions.

They think their pray are answered by repeating their words over and over, and again and again. Jesus said don't be like them, because God knows what you need before you even ask him.

They then told the people to pray like this.

Our Father: the description of the true, and living God which is the father of the Universe

Which art in Heaven: He is supreme, and where our Supreme God sits is on his throne, far above all.

Hallowed be thy name: We must shout his name without fear, but with boldness, don't wait for we know not the time nor the hour when thy kingdom come:

The word say he shall appear like a thief in the night, let us try our utmost, best to do what the word of God told us to do, and to live how he wants us to live. For thy will must be done in earth exactly, as it is in heaven: when we do his will on earth as it is in heaven he will definitely give us, from this day forth our daily bread: and because of our faithfulness towards the Kingdom God will open up and forgive those who had ever trespass against us: and not allow them to lead us into temptation by doing evil with them.

We have to be open up so God can deliver us from evil: the word gave us the assurance, that he is our shield and our protector, no matter what comes our way, he remains our shields, for thine Is the kingdom: every thing on earth and in heaven belongs to the Father who has power, and the glory: and this will be so forever and ever. May his Shekinah Glory his divine presence, fill up your dwelling place in Jesus mighty name.

Amen.

CHAPTER 26

And They Were Born

El Chuwl. God who give you birth. I got a revelation while waiting on my friend at the mall, while standing outside a store.

You were born, and oh what a cuddling time that was, with a cute baby on board. Everyone visiting to see this bundle of joy, while using remarks like, which side of the family the baby resembles, and who they might take after, what they might become in life, in the form of profession. That cutie turned one, pulling things, and the learning practice is the order of the day. You turn two, and three, here comes the Pitter Patter around the house, holding on to things, falling down periodically, and learning to rise again. Your parents now kisses and cuddle you, throw you up in the air, and admire every step.

They are now five years of age, and their words are forming a lot better. Now you here nope, with their little hands behind their backs, or their tiny body swinging left and right.

You are heading close to the teenage anger season. From cute to rude, answering back at times, or sometimes, not a word. Each day is a day older, heading into the twenties, about to walk down the isles and gaining a family of your own.

A husband and wife, with some kids are now in play, and age is being added on to your life one day at a time. Life is great, love is strong, kids are moving up in the lane of success. Fifty's is now knocking at your door with a vengeance, oh how time flies, when the fun has just began. Your kids are all grown, and are about to have a family of their own. Grandma, and grandpa are aching lately, with sore knees, and back pain at the forefront, lots of teeth are now missing. Arthritis has began to freeze you in place, and the oh and ah is being heard when you try to get up.

The gray hair is angry, and coming with a rage. You now start chasing every store, for what ever hair color or hats in site. Middle age is now obvious, and you are most slightly more on the outward than the in. Life becomes content, and appreciation for every day God favor you on earth reads thankful.

From their on out its really all God doing. Your vision gets dim, and squinting becomes permanent, but grateful you can still see. Hands shaking but determine to fight age like a bull, intending to go down strong.

Your movement becomes slow, and your walk shorter, but still determine to keep moving. One party beginning to get weaker than the other, allowing the grand kids to do as they please. Your grand kids start asking the questions, grandma/grandpa why are you always sleeping on yourself. With slow speech they answered, old age baby and a little weary.

The time comes, when one party left the other, with a shocking exit, being a realist and knowing, that this day would have eventually come in any case.

You discuss the deeds and wills, of who should get what. Then that time come to say good bye to the other. As the book of Ecclesiastes say a time to be born and a time to die, this we know is a surety thing.

And life starts all over again for someone else. We must realize, life is fragile, and technical, life is to be appreciated and cherished. Each and everyday should be enjoyed to the fullest, with joy and laughter consuming your lives.

Praise God daily, with hand lifted up in one accord, and sing blessed be the name of the Lord. And now it is one who stand alone, in grief, reflecting on the good old days if the mind is still active. Telling anyone who will listen about the partnership, and union God had blessed us with, and how wonderful a life they shared.

You now fill them up with wisdom and knowledge, that will be beneficial to their immediate and future life, and their family.

Then the time comes where one generation moves on, and another comes in, and the circle begins again.

While we are on earth let us appreciate, respect, love, care and reflect on each other, hug kiss and say I love you to each other, have regular talks, and never be ashamed of each other. Learn to compliment each other while being mindful, the other party would not have toned skin forever, real teeth, muscles, elasticity is almost gone, great eye site is replaced with glasses or contact lenses. A full head of hair, and a flat tummy is but a memory.

Learn to keep in mind life ups and, downs so when the denture comes to play with Fixodent, the hair color is really needed on a weekly basis, the tummy hangs with dimple and stretch marks, the hair starts shedding, the legs say hi with cellulite, the arms claps as you say good bye to someone, the bones speak while we answer with a grown.

The edge of your bed, becomes your favorite place to rise in the morning, where you can rest, and work the toes before stepping of.

The grocery cart is your good friends that you lean on. You head to an area of the house for something, and could not recall what you went for.

The dinner table becomes your naptime spot, after each meal, just remember always it was and it is all God doing and it is marvelous in our site, and generations to come.

As I push my glasses up from slipping down on my face, looking out through the bedroom window, awaiting my husband return home from work. I am reminded to always thank God for his goodness, mercy and grace he favored upon our lives, and say thank you Lord.

As of today we are 37 years in marriage, and with God grace I believe, he will add another 50 plus years on our life and yours, in Jesus name by faith Amen.

CHAPTER 27

Favor from the Enemy Seed

Although I have read the book of Samuel on many occasions, I some how never look at the book in this light, as I am viewing in now.

I recall, there is a certain fish that is called a Dolphin, and for years, people believe that fish was the best fish in the whole world, because the saying is, if a person was drowning, this fish will push you to safety. I want to say wake up, and be real, the fish never intended to save you, the fish just could not get somewhere sturdy to put you, so it can get a great grip and a morsel full. So it pushes until it gets to a rock, and when you get to the rock, by then its obvious, you will get up and walk off, leaving you with the mindset that is a real nice fishy.

If you waited a little more, you would have ended up on the dining table, on the rock, to be dinner for the fish.

David taught Saul meant well from the beginning like the fish, before he realize, what jealousy could do to a man, who were so loving at the very genesis of this union.

David was being push to the rock, to be eaten, but the master had a blue print, of what were to take place. Saul tried to take him down three times, the number three in the spiritual, is resurrection, but mercy said no!

In this parable, the rock really saved the man's life, but in the bible, it was Jonathan who God used to be David rock.

Who is the rock in your life? A rock is un shakable with no shifting, planted firmly in place.

This rock is unmovable. His name is Jesus Christ. No one, or nothing, can eliminate or destroy, that strength. Mighty conqueror, lion of Judah is he.

God is miraculously awesome. When he has a plan for your life, he will use even your enemy seed to save you. In this case the enemy seed was Jonathan. God will bring your enemy seed to your rescue, and at your foot stool, in the right time. In Jesus name. Amen.

Praise God.

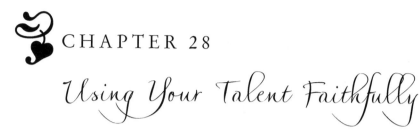

CHAPTER 28

Using Your Talent Faithfully

Directed towards the perfection, of what God has bless you women with.

God has blessed you with gifts, and these gifts I am speaking about now, is not pertaining to the gifts of the Holy Spirit. I am speaking about gifts, that is needed, to take you through your marital, and family life, to bring about a prosperous and successful marriage. You may ask what gifts I am speaking about?

You may even, say I don't have any, I am telling you today ladies, yes you do!

Who in the world, would be able to get up in the morning, start preparing breakfast, making sure your husband shirt and pants are in order for work, while the peculator brew the coffee, she gets back to the kitchen, set the table. While the family is having breakfast, you are peeking into one of the kids homework to make sure the questions in the math was done correctly. With a comb and brush in her hands, she combs her daughter's hair, then add the woggy. She then go over to the vitamin shelves, to be certain every one has what it takes to get them through the day. She kisses the husband good bye, and give him the lunch bag, wave to him from the front door, she then here outside, beep beep. The school bus is here, she raced out the front door, with their school bags and lunch kits, and kisses them good bye.

The door opens, and you enter the house to proceed with duties. Dish washer is being loaded, and laundry tumbling, vacuum running, knocking of pots and pans are the sound you here.

Vegetables is now being cut up, and meat is being seared for dinner, when you realize opps!, its 2pm, and the school bus is about to pull up outside your front door. Let me get into the shower were your words.

With hair still wet, you heard outside, beep beep. She runs to the door in her robe to greet the kids. Here comes some peanut butter, and jelly sandwich for snacks.

While they eat, she runs upstairs, and slip into a jeans and T shirt. Down stairs she heads to help with their homework.

The dryer lets out a sound, letting you know, the clothe is now dried. Ding dong, the door bell rings.

Here comes daddy, she plants that kiss on him, while asking him, how was your day honey?

Home work is done, and its time for dinner. Table all set, and now, cutlery knocking as chatting consume the room. After dinner, she loads the dish washer, then take the kids up to brush their teeth. She reads a Daniel in the lions den story Daniel 6:16, and tucks them into bed. Then she heads downstairs to fold the laundry.

With a glass of mild wine in her hands, she writes up the bills that's to be mailed off the next day. A swift snore he hears, as she dozes off with tiredness, and the glass in her hands is tilted.

Her husband wakes her up. She then empties her bladder, and heads of to bed.

The alarm clock chimes, its 6am, and the routine starts all over again.

I can go on.

Let me tell you now women, that's an anointed gift, and its

all towards the perfection of your family and using what God has blessed you with to do so.

Your husband will love you more, when he see your awesome techniques, of a great multitasking mother to his kids, and he will love you more, when you show him the interest, love, and care you have for him.

Most time we believe the word talent, is in preaching singing, on a podium, or being some TV star.

No! Your talent can be publicized right in your home. Start your ministry right where you are, in your home

Start using it now.

Your reward will be great. Because you just proved, you are an example of the Proverb -31 Woman and you are to be cherished. You are adorned with grace and anointing unmatched, with unique qualities, that you yourself did not realize, or recognize were fastened within you. You are woman, who's husband, and children rise up in return, and called you bless, Proverb 31:28. You were created by God, to add to the inadequacy of man, and to compliment each other. You are not an Idol, but a real woman, who are tuned in with her surroundings, and its needs, to bring perfection, ethics, and order within her household, and family, while being in the presence of the most high God. Now you can answer your own question. And I am sure the answer will be yes, I am extremely gifted. Celebrate you women, because you are deserving off the rewards that's arriving to your mailbox soon. Say thank you Lord in advance.

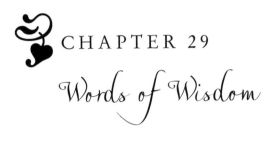

CHAPTER 29

Words of Wisdom

(1)- Noah build the ark before he saw the rain.
Don't wait to see a cloud, or a sign before you make plans, step in faith.

(2)-God uses different personality, to accomplish his plans.

(3)-The people in Genesis, were simple ordinary people. Through them God did great things.

(4)-Open your hands, and look closely at them.
You will see your gift written. Use it.

(5)-Don't be like the lepers, where only one came back to say thank you.
Never forget God goodness.

(6)-Let your life be as a sweet perfume, that where ever you passes, the scent of God anointing will leave a sweet aroma in the nostrils of others.

(7)-Submission is how you accomplish the mission. when you submit to your husband, you the wife is creating a spiritual atmosphere, of peace, love, unity, and God blessings, to enter your household.

(8)-You sow to the wind, you reap the world wind.

(9)-Beat your mountain with the word of God, and it will crumble

(10)-What is the space in your mind, 1x-2x-3x, or 4x.
What ever your size, that's the blessings you will receive,

(11)-Stop insulting God. Size it up.

(12)-Don't look for God in the big things only,
Look for God in the little things also.

(13)-Christian walk is like an adventure,
It looks like there no way its possible then, Bam There is always a way. Its never a dull moment.
There is always something along the walk to amaze you.

(14)-Parents be careful when you bring division into your home.
If you don't believe me, ask Rebecca, Jacob, and Isaac.

(15)-Women obey your spouse wisely.
If not it can dismantle a whole generation.

(16)-If you had no reference from the bible, where would we be.

(17)-Little is much when God is in it

(18)-What is your BMI?
B- Believe In God

M- Mission to serve
I- Intent to be more like God.

(19)-Sometimes it takes starting in your kitchen, or living room,
before you can sell out a stadium.
don't despise small beginning
Get excited about the grand finale.

(20)-We are people of faith, not people of fear.

(21)-Are you spiritually anemic?
Plug into the blood of Jesus Christ.
You will regain strength and power.

(22)-When you find you
Your have nothing to worry about.

(23)-Are you hanging out at the pool of Silom waiting on God?
Get up
You are already healed from sickness, Financial problem, and
more.

(24)- Do not fear giant that may be in your life now.
Be it Sickness, Homelessness, Finance.
Goliath was taken down.
Rejoice. The victory is yours.

(25)-When others try to shame you, have pity on them.
This means they are under arrest with shame in their own life.
Pray for them.

(26)-Stop compeering yourself to others.
You are uniquely designed, the form of no other,
If you don't believe me, ask your finger print.

(27)-Sarah laugh when she was told she will be pregnant. Bam. Here comes Isaac.
Be careful, your laugh may backfire on you for real.

(28)-Joshua approached the man asking
Are you friend or Foe?
He said neither
I am the Lord army commander. What Army are you in?Joshua 5:13

(29)-Be careful who you judge.
A prostitute Rahab, told the spies, we have heard how God made a path through the Red Sea
Even a prostitute heard about God, and took heed.
Selah! Joshua 2:10.

(30)-Activate your oxytocin, love each other, hug someone.
You never know, what they might be dealing with in their life.

(31)-Joshua choose 30, 000 fighting men, the key word is choose.
Choose your inner circle wisely, never be to thirsty for huge crowds.

(32)-You can rise from the ashes, and soar like an eagle.

(33)-You were praying for something and when it shows up you run.
If you don't believe me ask Rhoda - Acts:12:1:19.

(34)-Never take one person word and run with it,
Listen for the confirmation of 3 or more.
Also listen for God voice.

(35)-When negative words are thrown at you,
Worry not.

Sit back, lap your legs, sip a cup of coffee,
and watch God show up on your behalf.

(36)-Your tears won't always move God

(37)-Hurry birds do not build good nest

(38)-Marriage and love is a verb
Its based on doing.

(39)-It's time to call to order seriousness in the church, with no
compromising, delivering the word undiluted.

(40)-Be grateful for great family
Taking nothing for granted
Because you never miss the water until the well runs dry

(41)-Women learn to love yourself. Do not place yourselves on a
clearance rack, know your self-worth.

(42)-Marriage is like a bank,
what you put in is what you gets out.

(43)-Never allow a third party into your marriage, the only third
party should be God.

(44)-Marriage is permanent, parenting is tempory
When the kids leave home, you are both back to square one.
Alone
Never let that gap get to wide in your marriage.

(45)-When speaking to your partner, watch your tone
It helps to cease arguments.

(46)-A man with very little words does not mean he is angry, it means he is a king full of wisdom.

(47)-Never strive to win each other in an argument
kind words turn away wrath.

(48)-The key to a successful marriage is to serve God together.

(49)-Listen more, talk less, this does not mean you cannot share your opinion.

(50)-Be your spouse biggest cheer leader

(51)-In a relationship never expect miracles overnight.
Remember you are from two different background.
Learning each other takes time and patience which leads to longevity

(52)-The strongest marriage is being each other best friend, have humor, honesty, laughter, play, dance, and love hard, with no apologies.

(53)-There is strength in gentleness
Wives submit
Husband love your wives.

(54)-Allow your marriage to be like a vintage wine,
It gets better with age.

(55)-Who are called by God are qualified for the journey. Remain humble.

(56) Jesus did not whip the people in the street.
He whip them in the temple.(church)

(57)-A church is not where people go for entertainment
It's a serious place
It's a sacred place
Its you.

(58)-A mind that is void of peace and contentment, is the battle ground for the biggest war for which you cannot win.

(59)-You got to shift, as the target shift.
Can you hit a moving target?

CHAPTER 30

Women, Embrace Yourselves

My wonderful women, embrace yourselves, and accept your beauty. You may reflect on your youthful days, and how extremely lovely you use to look, elegantly adorned, and how brisk you use to walk, with a tiny waist line, long thick hair, great site and so much more

Listen!

You are still beautiful. You are still spunkadacious.

Now get up, shake that wig, and put it on. Take that denture out of the soaking glass, and put it into your mouth.

Get that cain out, so you can lean on it, let the cellulite flow, hook up that long line bra, pull that Girdle up, one leg at a time.

Embrace the drooping tummy, and the spear tires.

The feet that was once straight, is now K and swollen.

Just remember, it is getting you to your destination.

Get out your moisturizer, and apply it in an upward motion to the double chin.

Polish those nails, stick those eye lashes on, apply that lipstick, and limp in style. Slide up your mountain of victories.

Remember, you are daughters of the most high, and still remains God beautiful creation, and just in case some youth, or your children are laughing at you, remember this children. You are coming.

If you don't believe me check in the mirror, each year your birthday comes around. Acknowledge, while keeping in taught, they were once youths, who are so privilege, to grow into beautiful seasoned saints women

I say. Strike that pose, and live life to the fullest. Laugh heartily and love yourselves, with no apologies.

CHAPTER 31

Women, know your rightful place.

   MARY was at her rightful place, when Jesus rose on the third day. Luke -1:28

   Phoebe, was at her rightful place when
she answered the door, and Peter stood their.(Romans 16:1:2.

   Woman of few words (Mary of Bethany), was at her rightful place, when she anoint Jesus head with expensive perfume from the alabaster box.(Matthew -26:6:13)

   Martha was at her rightful place when she served at a feast to honor Jesus. Luke -7:36:50.

   Sarah was at her rightful place, when she was considered as a loyal wise woman, who did not give into fear.(Genesis 11:29:31.

   Deborah (means honey bee), was at her rightful place, when she became the First woman to lead an army while being a Judge -Judges 4:6:7.

Jael (Name mean mountain goat), was at her rightful place, to give the enemy Sisera warm milk, as he stumble into her tent for rescue from Barak and Deborah (Judges 4:21)

Naomi (Pleasant), was at her rightful place, when she return to Bethlehem with Ruth, who eventually marry Boaz, and gave birth to greatness.(Ruth:1)

Ruth (friendship), was at her rightful place, when she lay at Boaz feet. Ruth 2: 17. Boaz mother was Rehab.

Hannah (favor), was at her rightful place, when she pray like a drunk woman in the temple where Eli was, for a Baby. 1 Samuel -1:2:2:21

Michal (Who is like God), was at her rightful place, to moderate the drawn out battle, between Saul and David.1 Samuel 18:20:30.

Abigail (My father is Joy), was at her rightful place, to save Nabal her husband, from David sword. (1 Samuel: 25.

The Widow of Zarephath, was at her rightful place, when she bake a cake, and gave Elisha water, showing hospitality by faith.1 Kings 17:7:16

The Shunamite woman, was in her rightful place, when she show Elijah kindness (God Prophet)

Ester was in her rightful place, when she was chosen to be the next queen of the middle east. Ester 1:1:2:18

Proverb 31 woman, was in her rightful place, when she use wisdom, to keep her household in alignment.

The <u>Shulamite</u> woman was in her rightful place, when she use her voice, to speak directly to us in the scriptures. She boldly declares, her longing, and desire to be united to her lover in marriage. 2 kings 4:8:37

CHAPTER 32

Don't Pet the Snake

Suttle is he.

Trickster is he.

Evil is he.

Seeping, and crawling its way through life.

Was cursed from the very beginning, so he decided to try hard, at getting as much souls as possible.

Be very careful who you pet, in the form of friends, business partners, pushy persons, sly ones and so on.

You can be in line for a set up from the distracter. It is sad to say this, but its true, you may very well be

genuine and have lots of love, kind heartedness, with peaceful intent to share, but the snake you are petting has removed its skin, and it has other motives.

It crawls its way, sneaking into your lives, portraying innocence to the fullest, seeping as though it can hardly speak, pretending to be filled with humility.

Don't be fooled, or sidetracked. At times, their can be some genuinely good persons in your circle. Even so, you must never be to quick to adopt friends, unless you pray first.

God will give you the confirmation in your heart, then scan them for a while.

Never be in a rush, you may very well be petting a snake in a suit and tie, or well dressed in stockings, and high heels with lipstick.

Remember it can be very suttle, and won't care how long it takes. That snake will lay awaiting in the grass. It won't care how long it takes, he will wait you out.

Sliding pass your house, job, public place, for months, in some cases years, the snake in the grass does not care how long it takes.

He will take time out, and position itself in your path.

Be very vigilant not to step on its tail, the sting can be very sharp, and quick, you may not realize what bit you.

By then, it can very well be to late, their is no antidote for a petting snake poison.

Look out for the sad looks, and the pitiful personality, sometimes it's a trap.

Watch out for the devil in disguise, listen for the seeping tongue hollering at you, it's the enemy.

The snake can be in your company, and you might not recognize it due to its caring, helpful, concerning attitude. Be wise my ladies, go to the master for covering, protection, asking for site to recognize the fake petting snake crawled up, close to your feet pretending to be your pet.

Watch out for the crawl.

Its silent, the seep is quiet and the movement is swift. don't be fooled, by the petting snake. I now apply the blood of Jesus Christ over your life, your household, your family, your spouse, and your children. I pray your steps will be ordered by God, in Jesus name. Amen.

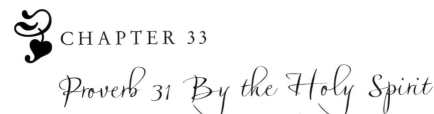

CHAPTER 33

Proverb 31 By the Holy Spirit

A virtuous, and capable wife is exemplary, she is worth more than rubies.

Rubies is known to be a very expensive piece of jewel.

It is a high energy stone, which is a type of sapphire. It is used to amplify energy. The ruby symbolized strength, and it was a favorite among the wealthy. It is known as a gem of passion, love and courage.

If you are worth more than that, this means you are in a category of high class.

It say in the word, her husband can trust her because of her capability as a wife, and in so doing she is showing of all she can do.

She handles things which greatly enriches his life. If you have a piece of jewelry as priceless as rubies around your neck, and you are in the company of others, automatically others will place you in a bracket of the rich and famous.

With her in his presence, the richness of her looks pulls her up to a high standard, where they compliment each other, that he also portrays an expensive and sophisticated look, that is part of how, she enriches his life. She will not hinder him but help him all his life. Because she is a brave and determined woman who pushes him into his purpose of excellence, and with her persistence she steps aside, as she pushes, so she will not hinder the path he has to walk through.

She works willingly with her hands, so he can be proud of her. She tries her hands at wool and flax, she sits not idlely by, but at all times keep prosperity in her household. Prosperity in your household represents blessings.

She is like a merchant ship, a merchant ship that carries cargo for business, and tons of goods that travels miles, and miles to bring food, this is her. The distance is never to far, or the load to heavy for her to get food, as long as it concerns her family. She is up early to prepare breakfast for her household, the most important meal of the day.

She makes sure her family starts on a good note, she is extremely capable and organized, that while breakfast is being made she plans her days work for her girls. A woman of business, there is little time spent on her behalf, getting their chores ready. Everything seems to be going right. She heads out to the fields to do her usual inspection, and if its up to her standard, she purchases the field.

As we saw she was a woman of class, and a rich one who had the power and authority, with a humble attitude, this was showing a magnificent picture of a wife with a noble and genuine character.

She did not just buy the land and leave it their, she plants a vineyard at once. You might question yourselves and ask why?

Its because she was an organized woman, that she knew she just spend a lot of money for the land, and instead of letting it lie around, she got it ready to bring in some monies at once, and that's wise.

Sometimes as women, you got to plough and rake into the blessing that you received immediately, and show your energy and strength, and your willingness to be a hard worker, even her helpers willingly triple up on their job in the field, because she set the example of being a hard worker.

She watches at the same time for more bargains, portraying the view of a rich woman.

As you read along, you see she was buying as long as she was getting great deal, fields upon fields, she bargains with the seller vigorously. We will assume after this hectic day she would drop dead beat into bed until next morning. No not her. As her light burns late into the night, she uses her hands in a busy way to spin thread, and twist fiber, you could see why this woman was so prosperous, and take pattern from her. This is what I perceive this to be. She was a woman who lends a helping hand to the poor an help the needy, the bible specifically taught us to give, and it will come back to you Luke 6:38. and this is exactly what is happening. Her blessings was flowing over, in full measure. Because she did not just receive and keep, she shared. Sharing is like a pitch lake, the more she takes out, the more it fills up. To me, it seems like the lake loves being extracted so it can receive more than it had before, that's a great feeling.

This proverb 31 woman had no fear of winter, because she was a lady who were always prepared. She prepares warm clothes, so as soon as winter leaves as we read in verse 22, she quilts her own bed spread, if you recall, a bed spread does not take one day to be done. This shows, she starts preparing really early. As women we ought to learn to prepared ahead of time in life.

When you rewind, and view Mrs. Proverb schedule we will believe she might have herself all dusty and untidy, pulling on a T shirt in the morning, with a skirt from under the mattress, or what ever her hand can grab, to begin her schedule for the day. Some might say, she had no time to be nice nice, pretty pretty, no. She took time out to dress like royalty ladies. In gowns of finest cloth, that means she was a woman of class, and elegance. She accepts nothing less than the best quality ladies.

You can positively say, she was a very influential lady with great character, who lots of women should be willing to take pattern from, and that is how we should be to our husbands. I am going to hit very hard here. Some women, their husband may have them under house arrest. Hiding them from the society, because they are not very public ready, and their class and stature, ethics, and quality may be very pore. Sometime instead of them being able to draw people near, they can be hired as human chaser for certain companies.

That is a sorry state.

When you read Verse 23, her husband is a well known man, who sits in high esteem in councils, with civic leaders. This is a high position he holds, she ought to be always ready, to back him up in a respectable and classy way. If women cannot be of great support to their husbands, and I mean support, in all his doing, then he will either get backing from someone else, or someone will be very willing and ready to support him in all ways (pause). Then you cannot say a word, because you left the door wide open, and as long as a door is open, its an invitation to enter.

When your husband holds high position, you ought to be side by side with him. This is what God meant when he said, two becomes one. You are now in one accord, with cords that cannot be broken, and I am saying here, some women becomes a disgrace to their husband. It may be in the way you speak to him, your dress code, the way you keep your house hold, what ever it is, its time to do some soul searching.

He might not physically speak it, but if you are wise as the bible taught us to be, also the Proverb 31 woman, you will be convicted at once. When this feeling captures your mind and heart, you will either start working on your marriage and situations, and do some reviewing of your whole married life, and see what is speaking back to you, and what's not. Then you should know what to do, to rectify circumstances before its to late.

She also makes belted linen garments, and sashes to sell to the merchants, this is really a woman of business that waste no time, clothed with strength and dignity, she laugh openly with no fear of the future. An extremely wise woman in her speech, which makes her and other women like her a plus to their husband

and society. She is a plus not a minus. His nose swells with joy, combined with an attitude of appreciation when she opens her mouth, some of our husbands cannot ever say this about their wives, as soon as their mouth open people will run or stand in shock to know, is that the wife of a prominent man. Wake up, and work on things and issues now. If you don't, who will. She portray kindness when she gives instructions, it is done in a stern but loving, and respectable way. She carefully watches all that goes on in her household and life in general. As women we should be watch dogs in and out of our homes, scanning scene, like a hawk. She is responsible, or will be held accountable if things do not go, or proceed right, in and out of her sorrounding. Visitors most times holds the woman accountable for the scene in general, and the way her home, husband and children is being kept. She is expected to be unique in the up-keeping of her belongings, and her business. She should not bear the consequences of being lazy, that's a bad stain to adopt. Never allow this

After all is said and done, will you be like the Proverb 31 woman ladies, where her husbands and kids stand to called her bless?

If your answer is no, my next question to you is, how bad do you want to rescue your marriage and family.

They called her bless, because she was an extremely outstanding figure, both in and out of the home. It was also extended towards her workers, she portrayed an openess of who she was, and is as an individual. She did not put on a mask, but possessed transparency of her as a woman.

Her husband honor and praised her, for she portrayed what God taught her to be, and how he taught her to live. A Virtous woman.

They are many virtous women, I will never say no there is not because there is.

But the bible in proverb say, this woman surpass them all. The word of God taught us and expects us to surpass the prophetes in the bible, with more knowledge than they themselves had, that means as women you are to accept this virtuousness, and open yourselves to receive the anointing to be better wives than she was, which means, you ought to press forward with excellence in all you do, say, and portray. Being a virtous woman means you got to be connected to the anointing, and are ready to be true ministers of your family. Before you proceed for a position on a podium chasing to be ministers, be ministers of your own house first, then other things will be added.

Why I say this, you may ask?, I say this based on experience, if you look at the schedule of the virtous woman, you will see without the Holy Spirit in her life, and without being anointed to serve, she would never, I say never ever had make it through.

If you slip into the carnal man. you will never be able to deal with a schedule as Mrs. Proverb 31. The word say charm is deceptive, and beauty does not last, but, a woman who fears the lord as God say in the word, when we fear God, it's the beginning of wisdom. I am sure she had a few flaws, but she dealt with them swiftly, because she feared God, that is why she was the best wife ever, she fear God, and that is why everything she touched, over flowed with great blessings, we can go on. Fear God women, and be what God has created you to be. Not for your husband, not for your kids, not for you, not for man in general but for God alone, and you shall be grately praised.

Its time to step forward ladies, and receive your prize. The prize of perfection, class, grace, excellence, diligence humility, love, and what ever else God sees needed, will definitely be added to you. After he prepares you for the task, my Proverb 31 sisters in Christ, he shall reward you for all you have done, and he publicly declears your praise when he is finish with you. You will never ever be the same again.

You will be in a anesthetic mode, where you will proceed to purpose, without feeling anything at that point and time. You will definitely know God is in your midst. God, bless you wonderful ladies. El Olam, the everlasting God.

Press on.

CHAPTER 34

From a Moth to a Butterfly

You go through life, in lots of different diversions.

Some go through a horrific life, some a cell life, and some a corrupt life.

I realize you go through all these things, when we do not put God in our lives first, sometimes some was never taught about the goodness of God, some deliberately don't want to know, and some wickedly hate the name of Jesus Christ.

Can I say right here and now, we can go ahead and settle for a life like the moth, who can be ugly at first site. I have never seen a gorgeous moth at its inception.

This illustration can relate to, a life of hurt and frustration, depression, sickness, single family home, divorce, homelessness, and more. This can turn your life into a moth misery, so ugly, you yourself could not imagine, where and when you got to that state.

I would like to say to you, without the master God, and savior Christ Jesus you will be nothing, and continue to be nothing. I call this dead man walking.

There is only one way to escape the scare of what life throws at you. Be willing to allow God to be your pilot.

All your life, you controlled the pilot of your own life, and situations, and you may have messed up. somewhere along life path way, but who has not. You have very little excuse now. You cannot touch problems, and prosper, it may seem prosperous for a second, but somewhere down the road, you will meet that brick wall of hurt, suicide, depression, sickness and lots more.

You might never be able to escape, unless you turn your life around. you must be determined in your mind, that you are totally tired of being a moth, crawling around all day, with the same movement all your life, of setbacks, disappointments, stumbling blocks, hurdles, puddles and a total halt of progress in your life. Its time to change your position.

The moth could have, settled for staying in that same old sorry state, but it did not, and you should not either. You have more advantage over the moth. Take authority, and move into your rightful place.

You have the privilege, to know the God of beauty. As a butterfly has beautiful colors, and flaps its wings gracefully, with no problem in the world, just as the fly glides freely, high above situations that can harm it, the same way your life can be changed, from the Moth, to a butterfly.

All you have to do is release, and rest on God, you can trust whole heartedly without fear, and without thinking, you are going to change back into the old cocoons. This is all up to you. Don't allow yourself to accept residency, in the world of the Moth again. Its up to you. Give the Lord and Savior Jesus Christ a chance in your life. He is the one who transforms you, and the way to receive that transformation is to allow the Holy Spirit to take precedence in your whole being. Empty yourself of the world, and make yourself available, to be filled up with the Holy Spirit who will do the work within you.

This whole transformation has to do with how bad you want this change.

It has to do with desperation, it has to be you, and knowing where you are, and where you want to go from here.

It must be, you and only you. Tired and exhausted of resting in the same crawling, colorful way of life.

Push through, to that dimension, where you are willing to surrender all, that is where you will change, into the beauty God has created you to be.

This is where you will be ready to accept the change of freedom in Christ, that is where the butterfly in you will be revealed.

Lift up your wings and fly my queens.

CHAPTER 35

Going Through The Plateau Period!

The Plateau periods of life can be very challenging at times, but keep in mind who is your head liner. His name is Jesus Christ. First of all, the word Plateau comes from the Geology and earth science, described as a steep mountain, with a flat or level top.

This Plateau period can be define, as a time where little growth, hope, or development in life happens.

Yes.

Do not allow your heart to skip a beat or two, because I use this remark (little growth or development). It do happen, to the best of believers in Christ.

You are also human being, who do go through at times, while wearing it well. Beautiful ladies of God remember this, you have an edge over the people of the world, his name is Jesus Christ, your head liner who gave you free access to him. The earth quaked, the rocks split, and the veil was torn in two - Matthew 27:51, that you can take the whole bundle of situation, and circumstances, fold it up neatly, add a bow to it, and turn it over to Jehovah. When you have that confidence, your garden will be watered again with unlimited overflow, while the Holy

Spirit prepare saturate, and grow uncontrollably, with mighty weight, of peace, joy, and wealth following.

Again, this will only happen, when you totally, and vigorously let it all go. Let it be like a fire that burns within like Jeremiah 20:9. God will strengthen you just in case a plateau season comes around again. It don't have to necessarily loiter around for a long time. Let the creator of pray faith hope confidence authority be your guide daily.

For you have a helper, Protector and Shield in Christ. This is the facts.

CHAPTER 36

The Auction Sale

Have you Ever imagined being auctioned off to the highest bidder, that you felt so betrayed, while at the same time thinking, the whole world is also against you.

Even your own family, and blood relatives plots against you, that's the deepest hurt their can be. It may have happen to you, and you felt really sad, My friend listen to this, I want you to get ready, prepare for the Joseph Season you might be stepping in to. When God has favor upon your life, no man can hinder you, no matter what or how they try.

Once you were ordained by God, no blockage can occupy that space in your path.

His brothers taught they had him now, but that was a lie from the pit of hell, or should I say from the pit. It all started in his boyhood days, being the favorite in the eyes of his father Jacob. So favored, that he was known to be the son with the coat of many colors. Genesis 37:1:10

His father Jacob made Joseph a beautiful coat, because their was so much love between the two. They always had a great communication, and the other brothers detest him. They hated Joseph, and planned to make his life miserable.

Its not every dream you need to share, or expose to certain

individuals, because everyone will not be mature enough to handle the information.

At that point and time, Joseph did not know this, and it was not for him to know. When God has his hands in the mix, take your hands off.

Joseph left one day for the fields, which he will eventually own. But at that time, it did not look so. He met his brothers, who already saw him coming from a distance, and plot to kidnap him, some plan to even kill him, but like everything in life, there is always someone who will eventually look out for you. One of his brothers Reuben, said to the others, lets throw him into the pit, their must be one to boycott the others.

You see, if they throw him into the well, he Reuben will eventually go back and get Joseph out, and eventually, he can be looked upon like a great hero.

Never the less, you must realize, this was a set up from God of what's to come. Sometimes you will have to stay put in the pit, but for a little while, keeping in mind, to step forward, you must not wiggle (stay put), and stand still, if you twitch to much you can sink deeper. Joseph was sold to the highest bidder that day at the auction sale, because he fitted the description of a robust built slaves. Sometimes in life when you are being auctioned to the highest bidder, you must be still, and keeping in mind, God is in control..

His brothers sold him for twenty pieces of silver, ten less than Barabas sold Jesus for, and they went their merry way, with premature happiness within. Believing they had accomplished something, but they had another thing coming, and the story went on.

I want to let you know, sometimes, along life journey, you will have to sit in the well for a moment, then you might have to rest in Egypt for a little time, and while in Egypt, you may have to work ridiculously hard, use it as a form of physical exercise. Their you will be getting yourself in shape, to handle the blessings God is sending your way.

Don't give up, when you are near to the victory line. You might have to face the Pootiphar season of sabotage, lies and even imprisonment, use that time to elevate yourself in the word.

Lets call it the jail cell university of Theology, and if you are familiar with theology university, you will know it takes two to four years to be completed, hallelujah.

At times you will be ask to interpret dreams, the holy spirit will prepared you for such time. And when the harvest time is upon you, leap into your victory break through. I must remind you, when you get there, its not over. A famine will come, but the beauty is, you will be in charge, and in the position to lead. Do not call them wicked, because when God has a plan for your life, that is the path he will take you through, before the praise of victory comes. He will use even your goliath to lead you to the finish line.

Enjoy your walk through the auction sale season, because when you exit your season of drought, you will enter into your barley harvest season.

Don't shine before, wait until the light is spotted directly upon you, and then shine bright like no light have ever shined before.

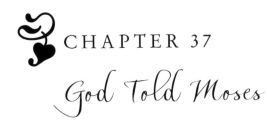

CHAPTER 37

God Told Moses

God told Moses in Exodus 4:17, be sure to carry staff, so you can perform miraculous signs, and wonders

My question to you is, do you have your staff at all times with you?

You are hindering your own progress, when you stand alone in all you say and do.

The word teaches, his Rod and Staff not might, but will comfort you always.

Be sure the storms of life situation, or circumstances do not catch you unprepared. Equip yourself with your heavy artillery, the bible.

If you have that weapon, in the form of your staff you will have no reason to fear. Go to your bookshelf, and dust that sword clean, and begin to read.

Their is strength, power, healing and victory, in the staff who comforts you.

Hold up your staff now. The bible and say I have confidence and I believe. You will prove, the staff is the true and living word.

CHAPTER 38

Word of Wisdom and Reflection

1-Bask in the joy of your expectations, for when your expectations come, the joy will be short live.

2-A mind that is void of peace, and contentment is the battle Ground for the biggest war for which you cannot win.

3-You cannot keep your aim in the same direction while the target moves. You must, shift with the target.

4-Enjoy the journey, for the joy in the journey is better then the joy of reaching your destination.

5-The truth is a long term investment that pays good dividend.

6-<u>Do not if or maybe God.</u>

7-Finance solve problems, but do not make you happy. Many rich divorced couples would gladly exchange their money for a good marriage.

8-Lasting relationship don't just happen
You must work on it.

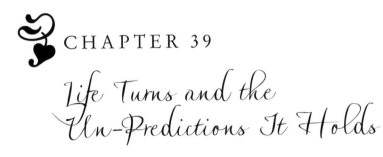

CHAPTER 39

Life Turns and the Un-Predictions It Holds

The family.

We are born into this world, through great parents, and it is the happiest time in a families life. You cuddle, and love that baby to the max, and cherish them, but as time goes by things changes.

It sometimes alter the atmosphere for the better, or may have an un-predictable turn ahead.

After all the love that child received, comes to a halt, they may have to proceed on their own, along life pathway, weather they are prepared, or not. Just thinking about this, brings tears to my eyes.

You might ask yourself why?

This is why.

The child now moves on, to face the world on their own, and that is where the children really needs guidance, but never receives it, due to the hectic busy lifestyle that fills the atmosphere. They are sent out in the world, with no experience, on how to take care of a home, prepare a proper meal, do their own laundry, spend their finance wisely, and learning when to put priority first. What a pity. At the most tender stages of his or her life, they are left in the wilderness. In that phase, a lot can happen. They are exposed to the wilds, and the elements of this world, un prepared, just thrown into the den of the devourer, waiting in many form to shred them to pieces.

This can be in the form of a praying mantis (men), so called friends, and in some cases these days, the place of worship, also on the job.

When you run and bump constantly into walls, erected by bricks, where there is no way out, no one to speak life into this young person, who eventually grows into an adult, and you are not able to stand, what will you do, and what choices will you make.

A mirage situation, that might be confusing to you, giving you a negative reading. By then, you have been through so much, but seeing no victory sign in site. Your dreams seems shattered from where you are standing, and the efforts you have sown into trying to make life worth while, shows you its rear view. Your desire and dream of a happy home and family, at some point and time in life has slipped away. Now you are left standing alone, depending on God grace and mercy to hold your hands. With your persistence, and by never giving up, here comes a breakthrough. Just say thank you God.

Then, here comes another hurdle (stage), while you are in the blessing zone, you sit back, and start viewing it all over again, from the outer, and inner circle of your past and present life, and these words arrest your mind, if only I knew.

Water now flows from your eyes, thanking God for where he brought you from, keeping in mind, what could have been, If only you had someone speaking words of wisdom into your life, that would have molded your life. Trust and believe, it is not to late, and never allow that taught to invade your mind and space. That is a plot of the devil. Blot him out, keeping in your heart and mind, God is a restorer of all you have lost. He will deliver it back to you, in triple portions, press down and shaken together. Weeping may endure for a night, but joy comes in the morning.

The hills, and valleys of life had to come, in order to get you to this dimension you are in today. It may have lead you to the most ill taught, and frustrated feelings. When you look in the distance, visualizing, that there may never be a way out, and no hope is in site, remember, in life there is always a door with a key, and that key is the Lord and savior Jesus Christ. The ordeals of life package is now sealed, and a new package is opened. Just receive in Jesus Mighty Name. To my wonderful parents, who were blessed with your quiver full of kids, I say this, exercise the teachings of God word in the bible, and follow with seriousness, and a little tough love. This will prepare your kids to face this world that will not be forgiving, when the time comes to scold them with hate, and then spew them out. Make a necklace, with the scripture of God, and place it around their necks. Proverbs 22:6. That reads. Train up a child in the way they should go. Remember, they are the future generation of tomorrow. God entrusted them into your hands, and you will have to be accountable to him in the future. Here is where you can ask yourself this question, have I done a great job? You can answer this yourself. Cry today when you scold them, or cry tomorrow when the world devour them.

The choice is yours. Never allow these words to exit your mouth, if only I knew.

You have the power after God to take control of your own home parents. Dry your eyes, for the oil of joy is paying a visit to your home. You have another chance to set your house in order, Isaiah 38:1. So when the time comes for your wonderful children to step out into the world, they will be prepared to the fullest. Then you can bless them with joy, instead of fear and tears. And feel extremely proud of your finished products, your children.

Just receive in Jesus mighty name.

Amen.

CHAPTER 40

The Jail Break

Situations go and comes in our lives, and we sit and ponder things that means nothing, or will do us no good, without realizing, who we serve, and who holds our future.

When people of God looses that vision, of the high calling it allows that focus to disappeared. Then we are situated in a place of venerability, and that is playing in to the evil one hands.

We must at all timed stand firm on the word, and use it with authority. God gave us the (Dunamis)power to use the word, you have the authority to do so.

When you read the word, you can see where prophets and men of God worry not, because they knew, what ever came there way, it will turn out for the best.

Rewind a bit, and view the season of acts. When time drew near where Peter would be imprisoned, they had no fear, one thing you need to realize is, these men were chastised, and was treated cruelly to the fullest, but they held out, knowing it was all for a purpose, and the purpose was Jesus Christ.

They held out, and took what ever came there way, because there were coming a time, where their will be the biggest Jail Break in the history of the world.

The first jail brake ever to have taken place. Peter, God

disciple, was a man of God, and a man of faith, who listen to the voice of God and obeyed, and act on it. These were men who put God first, in everything they did (James and Peter).

When the time had come which they had already know will be coming came, they were both arrested, in the first place, some of you would not even bother to proceed, in doing the will of God, because of fear. But they knew, fear is not of God, so they held out, by standing on their belief, and love for the Lord.

They went willingly to their cell. and while there they prayed and sang all night. The time came, when King Herod of Agrippa sent for the first apostle James and had him killed by the sword, never the less James already knew, and was prepared for what's to come, so he went willingly, knowing for sure, he was going to a better place, heaven.

When you are positive about your faith, you should have no fear for what's to come, because you lived the life God commanded you to live, and you did it In spirit and truth, so transferring from the earth realm, to the Heavenly realm will be a peaceful one.

While all this was taking place, the followers were in their secret temple praying, for the release of peter. They prayed all night, sometimes you need to keep your eyes open, while lifting up Jesus all night long, none stop, like the followers of Peter did.

The night just before Peter was tried, he were asleep in the cell, and chained between guards and soldiers, with other guards at the prison gate, no matter where you are chained, there would come a time, where you will be released. As long as you continue to keep the word of God in your heart, without keys as long as it's the will of God you will be free.

That night the cell was engulf with, a bright light. Suddenly, the angels of the Lord stood before Peter, little did he know it was jail break time. In the wee hours of the night, the angel tapped peter on his side to awake him, and said to him, quick, get up.

And the chains fell of his wrist.

All that time, the Lord had already put the guards into a deep anesthetic sleep, so Peter put on his sandals, and got up quickly, the angels told him to follow, even Peter was unable to handle the jail break, he taught he was still in a dream, even though the angel was leading him out, he still thought it was a dream that he admitted in the Bible. Although Peter and all the others were combing the earth preaching the good news of our Lord and savior, whom we serve letting them know about the marvelous miracles, he still taught it was a dream. Never the less, he was leaving the jail in royalty.

Escorted in fine style in the spiritual realm, what a mighty God we serve. When God delivers, he does not proceed in a mediocre fashion, he does it with uniqueness.

Even though the followers were praying all night, they to was in a frenzy when they saw Peter at the door, that they left him standing there, and run inside the temple. That Rhoda is something.

They were praying with such power, that the Jail Break of the century took place, and they themselves could not even believe.

I want to urge you, As long as you read it in the spiritual encyclopedia of life, the Bible, you can live it because its real as can be. If God can allow, and give the ok for a Jail Break, he can do anything, and he can do it just in time, because he is a just in time God. We see he did not show up before a certain period, he was on time, that is when the time was perfect.

We must not force a point, for things to happen before time, because you can delay the process, and plans God has for you. While you wait sing a song, read the word, that will keep you occupied. There is coming a time, when God word is all we will have to live with and depend Until it's time for the jail break.

Let the word be marrow to your bones, and wear it in your heart.

CHAPTER 41

God Has a Plan for You or the Devil Would Not Be Tempting You

While sitting, and inhaling the view of everyday life, you start speaking to yourself.

No matter what people might be saying, be it, you are crazy or you talk to yourself, close them off, and focus on your daily life.

See if this is what you had planned for your life, when you were young, and I believe your answer will most definitely be no. Not this.

You start rewinding, the plans of your youth which now looks like a puzzle. You try hard daily to believe, keeping in taught, you may never get out.

To my dear sisters and brothers, remember this always, feel your own greatness without expectation of others. Those plans are not expired yet, and don't allow anyone to tell you different, especially the devil.

God plans are enormous and gigantic, not easily banished or deleted from the book of the masters plans. When you realize, and believe this, you will recognize why the devil is on your back daily. Its to try and make you believe, your life is unstable, and age is creeping up on you, you lost a few teeth and put on enormous amount of weight, he makes you feel all your hair are swiftly becoming gray. Keep remembering this, there is all different brands of hair colors and fixodent to keep the denture in place, so nothing he can or will stop the plans of God. If your hair starts shedding, bond that weave on.

The devil throws these things at you, to distract from the prize God has for you.

Do not turn away from his promises, and the word that accompanied, cementing the confidence he has sown within you. God wants you to stand firm without any shifting.

The plans God has for you makes the devil hate you, he hates you with a passion, and you have to be able to identify this. Start pressing through to the promise, to the blueprint God has for your life.

Its never to late, don't ever believe that lie. it is a trick from the pit.

Sit down now, and take notes of the plans that was in your mind that was stolen, and take it back. Bring it forward to the front of the line, and present it to God. Always keep in mind, God already knew, but this will assure him you are ready. Break free from the chains of delayed blessings, and rest directly to the front, where you are lined up to say present please. I am reporting for duty Master.

God will put the devil in his place, the pit of hell in Jesus name. Never fear, when you know definitely, God is on your side, that is the most secure feeling you can ever have.

As long as you maintain that positive mood and confident, God is in control.

Take precedence on the promises of God, and trust him totally, and you will realize he is beautiful beyond description.

CHAPTER 42

Anointed to Serve

God has given you a dutiful task, as mothers wives and, best friends of your homes.

It is a great responsibility, and privilege to be awarded these duties by the most high God. This is the only certified position, that you will not receive a doctorate, mba or certificate for. It is an on the job training, that is learned extremely quick, with professionalism and developed skills embracing.

The duties may seem heavy, tiresome, and burdensome to carry at times, allowing discouragement, and despondent feelings to reside.

I am telling you today ladies, never ever be tired or weary, that is a lie from the pit of hell.

As women you can handle more than you can imagine, and to top it off, you were anointed to serve in the home and where ever needed. You are multitasking machines in human form. Here is where you give yourself a round of applause, it's a well deserved.

You are daughters of the king, and he place you in a royal position, in an area of managing your home. You are the domestic goddess, and that is a title most persons cannot attach, to their resume.

Do it with love, pride and dignity. The enemy will try to

frustrate you, and put negativity in your ear, but never forget, you are called to serve. Put these things into practice, and see a magnificent turn around in your household. Do not be sensitive to every word spoken. Forgiveness, is a life long process. Always make time for your spouse, and kids, looking out for their needs before personal activities after God. Marriage is permanent parenting is temporary, when the kids leaves home, it all comes back to you and your husband. Do not let that space draw to wide. The only third person in your marriage should be God. Lasting relationship do not just happen, you must work on it. Never use negative words towards each other. Speak life into your king, and expect the same to be directed to you in return. Marriage is like a bank, what you put in is what you get out. Use wisdom, before the brain engage the mouth. Time is precious, and should be spent with each other in love and unity at all times. Spend wisely, the most problem in a marriage arrives due to the lack of finance. Watch your tone. Kind words turn away wrath.(Proverb 15:1). Have patience with each other, Ruth went low when she was at Boaz feet that is called submitting, and she went high when she married him. Pray to be lead by the Holy Spirit, to give you wisdom. Let your marriage portray, the fruit of the Spirit at all times, Joy, Love, Peace, Kindness, Goodness, Gentleness, Self-Control, Faithfulness. Continue to keep your eyes on Jesus, looking neither left nor right but straight ahead, and you will see, your reward will be enormous with no regrets. In life, you must first show love, so it can come directly back to you. Its like throwing a ball at the wall, you throw good, it will come back to you, you throw bad, that to will come right back to you. Misunderstanding will happen at times, be sure to sort it out before bed, or church, let the light that shines through you be honest and truthful to God and man. Successful marriages, and homes, comes through great communication, submission, love. and respect. These practices should not be a burden, and pressure, because, they are all laws of the bible, and God word towards us. Now, put that lipstick on, apply that eye shadow, place that eye liner on, and smile with love, glowing through, as you proceed to being as a distinguished woman, who are unique, and beautiful in your own rights, and gifting. Let the anointing and wisdom lead. You have untapped strength. Do not be afraid to tap in. Here is where you shout, thank you Jesus.

CHAPTER 43

Power in the Handkerchief

A hand kerchief can be used, as a form of blotting sweat, for style or a head tie, and when you are finished you toss it aside, or into the wash.

Did you ever think or imagine, what power that hand kerchief may hold?

In Acts 19:11, God gave Paul the power to do miracles through the Hand Kerchief or cloth, that when it touched his skin, and were placed on the body of others, they were healed of their diseases, and any evil spirits within them came out.

That is power, in the hand kerchief.

Power were not offered to Paul alone, it was for all of God children who believe, and have faith in the true and living word.

Lets make our selves available to the most high, Lord and savior Jesus Christ, to be used, while allowing the anointing he has given, you to arrest our hearts soul and mind. You must be women with your Hand Kerchiefs always in hand, ready to touch with power and anointing, through the Mighty Master God our father.

Get your hand keys anoint it, and always, keep it as a point of contact like Paul did, in Jesus Name

Be sure to pray first, and wait to receive permission from the Holy Spirit, for the next move. You will feel a shift within, that will agitate you to get your handkerchief.

Amen.

CHAPTER 44

Women of Purpose

Never give up, and never toss in the towel.

Never Accommodate or entertain Rejection

You eventually learn, to appreciate what God has in store for you after a delay, when things you desire desperately do not happen in your timing. You might be so depressed, and frustrated at times, allowing different thought to roam through your minds, that are most times negative. Very rear its the positive.

Know this now, a delay in life means a victory is ahead.

You will definitely learn, when God is in control you should never ever worry. Because Jehovah Jeirah never gives us a unprofessional, or half way blessing.

He is a perfectionist, in all he does. When you have a cake in the oven, if you remove it before time it flops (fall), it must stay in the oven for the full time. When its completed, you will have the most tastiest cake their can be, wait. Never be in to much of a haste.

When that blessings comes, it will be in a marvelous and unique order, that you forget the frustrated moments that were before you, focusing on the blessings it self.

This shows you, it's time wasting, and mind bugging when you sit by, and stress yourselves over something that may never happen. Instead, we should keep focus on the planner himself, the Lord and Savior Jesus Christ, and watch him exhumed everything that was sealed, placing them in its perfect way, place and time for your lives. You sometimes look at others around you, and their success in life, and get despondent but know this. Your vitamins may not work for someone else, and someone else's vitamins may not work for you. Adopt your own techniques, and uniqueness, that is not matched to another. Never be a carbon copy of someone else.

The Alabaster box was broken. Pass your hands in the ointment (Perfume), that was spattered, when the box was broken. The broken box of no job, finance, sadness, illness, homelessness, and anoint yourself, as you walk into your greatness towards your next dimension. Pray vigorously with passion, and desperation for Christ and fast in secret, and if you loose hope along life walk, that may frustrate you at times, remember, the amazing hope, is Jesus Christ who never leave you nor forsake you. Allow your confidence to be the omega, will lead you towards greatness. Now sit back, lap your legs, sip on a cup of coffee or hot cocoa and look at God work.

CHAPTER 45

Tears

<u>Woman:</u>

Homeless, but still demands her respect, of being a mother on call, without a husband, with children to care for, living out of her car, because she lost her home. Her bathroom is a bucket (Pale), and a wash cloth to give her kids a quick clean.

With pride and love beaming from her face, as she dresses her kids, placing her arms around them, with her head bowed, but being held high with pride.

She knew without a doubt, all things are possible, and her situation and circumstances, are just for a little while.

She shed enough tears, and its now time to wait upon the Lord for her miracles, and delivery to come forth.

<u>Man</u>

Feeling less than a man, who lost everything in his path

His wife and kids are gone, his home and car gone, bank account at zero.

Walking by, he came upon a soup kitchen. He step in with tears in his eyes. Tears of hunger, tears of gratitude, for those who provide to the needy persons. He step in with tears in his eyes, but came out with joy in his heart.

For his empty stomach, is now filled. Praise God.

Naked
She step in stride, with pride, but no one knew it was her only outfit.

With class, she never hangs her head down, but wear it well, she washes, it iron it, and wear it again and again

She never allowed anyone to recognize her tears.

She step out with a positive look, with rubber bands as bracelets, safety pins for earrings, and Vaseline as lip gloss. With confidence, she walked in stride, believing what God promise will come through.

She dry her tears, and wait with humility.

Hungry
Tummy respond with a growl.

Upset stomach, eyes dim, and voice saying, if only I can get a morsel to eat.

Wondering why Lord.

Why others have in abundance to their disposal, and some have not even a pinch to eat.

Faint and weak, I feel in deed, but cant help their selves.

For no one cares about me. They are filled to the brim, and burp with strength, but I am left to swallow my saliva.

With tears in their eyes, a question was ask, did they not remember God word?

Feed the hungry.

I pray, fill me Lord with spiritual, and physical food, that I may gain strength to perform the duties you have commissioned me to do.

Child
Help, oh Help, me with my little tattered, and torn life.

Weak, and snotty nose, weeping for my tummy hurts,

Lack of meals day and night.

Will someone please help me?

My feet are bruised, for lack of shoes, my clothes tattered and torn. With busted hands, cold, bleeding and paining.

My tiny body shaking, and palms turned up, all stripped.

Her mouth mumble, Lord, what did I do to deserve this.

With tears in her eyes, she said, my childhood in action seems like there is no end in site.

My only continual hope is in God

Wife

Who would have known, this would be my lot.

Hey sweet heart, what beautiful eyes, coke shape body like I have never seen, was his words.

Lips are like cherries, and hair flows with natural curls, were all words exiting his mouth.

Trusted was her to fall for those flowery words.

Hands stretch forth accepting, and believing, I agreed to take his hands in marriage.

Step with head held up high was I.

Little did I know, as the ring was round so was the marriage.

Full circle of hell begins. Day one, hugs and kisses

Day two, dumb founded was he.

Day three, where is my food woman, she heard

Day four, remember you are my slave.

Day five, why is my pants not ironed.

Day six, put some pep in your step woman.

Day seven comes, she is wearing shades in the house, day and night.

Day eight jump back, and start all over again.

But God plus tears, equals victory.

She has hope, and belief, that God will lead the way.

She embraces a vision within, of a sign that reads,

From sadness to joy.

I plea with you, to assist the less fortunate, as much as you can, always keeping in mind, the commands God gave to us as believers. Connect the word of God, to your everyday life, in obedience love, and wisdom.

I pray the fire of God blaze upon you real good, and may you receive, what you hand out to others, in full measures press down, and shaken together. May your household be overflowing with a Tsunami of blessings in Jesus mighty name. Amen.

CHAPTER 46

The Successful Family

From the Holy Spirit.

Have you ever wondered, or ask yourself the question, how can you maintain a good, and loving family.

Proverb 12:24 and 17:26 says:

Work hard, marriage is an investment.

What you put in, you will definitely get out.

Proverb 18:17 - Listen before answering

Proverb 18:15 - Be open to new ideas

Proverb 18:5 - Stand up under pressure, don't go down.

Proverb 27:21 - Stand up under praise.

If you put those ideas into practical things, you will definitely see changes in your home.

Marriages is the journey you must take together to bring about a successful family, husband, wives and align themselves into a special union, which has contour the basis for a great family.

Stop a while, and look each other in the eyes, and say, what is marriage?

Some might be saying, you don't know, and some will be saying, marriage is the joining together, of a man and a woman in a special union, and you will be perfectly right.

God join the two party together, because he saw something in you, that would be capable and ready, to handle the responsibilities, that comes along with marriage.

Such as kids, managing a home, and bringing forth the real example, of what a family should be.

Don't disappoint God. Take the package that was given to you, in the form of the vows, and oath you have taken and use it.

Invest in your family, and view your account as time goes by, you will see, the interest gained is beyond your expectation.

Joshua 24 - Joshua was specific without compromising the word of God, he said as for me and my house, we will serve the Lord, and his household was blessed.

In order for you to maintain blessed, and exemplary families, you must use the word of God at all times, to pilot your every day family lives.

In today's world, where marriages are often taken lightly, or twisted into something God did not intended it to be, keep focus on the bible teaching, and all about marriages.

Its extremely important.

The family is the bedrock, and its compulsory you live the way God designed it to be.

Pleasing him totally, and adopting his teaching on marriage.

<u>What the Bible say about Marriages.</u>
Genesis 2:18:24 - Marriage is God Idea
Genesis 24:58:60- Commitment is essential to a successful marriage
Genesis 29:10:11- Romance is important
Jeremiah 7:34- Marriage holds time of great joy
Malachi 2:14:15 - Marriage creates the best environment, for raising children
Matthew 19:6- Marriage is permanent
Romans 7:2:3- Only in death, should a marriage dissolve
Ephesians 5:21: 33- Marriage is based, on the principled practice of love, not on feelings.

Ephesians 5:23:32- Marriage is living

Hebrews 13- Marriage is good and honorable, good marriage produces great family. Put these things in to action. Their will be less divorces taking place, and more long term marriages will remain in place. Be vigilant of the enemy, who is desperately cruel, and heartless when it comes to destroying your house hold, and upon your family members. Be sure to always have your equipment on hand, frank incense and myrrh oil, and anoint your family, in Jesus mighty name.

May God bless your family.

CHAPTER 47

Inspiration Given by the Holy Spirit

God sent the storm into the ocean upon Jonah, for a reason (Jonah 1:14).

He got punished, due to his disobedience. Jonah realized what was taking place, and in order for the storm to cease, he ask the sailors on the ship, to throw him over board.

The sailor eventually comply to Jonah request. He told them to, pick him up and throw him over board, for if they did not, the storm will proceed, and their lives would be in jeopardy..

Sometimes in life, we need to make a decision, when its time, to throw excess baggage over board, and when its necessary to change position, while recognizing what God is saying to you. He will go that far, to get your attention.

The choice is yours. Either you take time, to do what the master is saying, or stay in the belly of the fish, until the third day.

How marvelous is God. Even the fishes of the sea, obeyed him. The fishes followed his plans, and they connected with God on, when they should make the next move. Keep the attention totally on him, not only in body but in taught, so that your pray shall be earnest.

The fishes knew the voice that ordered them, when time came around to spit out Jonah. The fish obeyed.

There are times in life we must remain attentive and alert, so when a word comes across, we will be sensible enough to hear and obey.

You might need to remove your earthly crown, and get into Sac cloth and ashes.

When I look further on, I saw where God speared the city, after they took heed. Guess what.

Even the animals were ordered not to eat a mussel of meal, everything and everyone in there, midst fasted.

Wow.

We need to take pattern from the book of Jonah, and see what became of him, when he did not obey the Master, and what could have happened if he did.

Something to ponder on.

God may very well be speaking to you individually. could it be, there is a spirit of disobedience in your life, in your marriage, at your job, even in your spiritual life. I pray you take heed.

May God Bless you in your obedience.

CHAPTER 48

Twice to Born, Once to Die

While getting dress for work one morning, this revelation came to me.

Twice to born, and once to die.

I then ask the question, why twice to born, and once to die Lord?

I then realize, this revelation was coming from the Holy Spirit.

We all were born out of our mothers womb, in the physical realm into sin, because the word of God teaches us, we were born into sin, and shape in to Iniquity.

Therefore, birth came from the beginning of time, and it was and still is a blessing from God.

He told us to be fruitful, and multiply, and replenish the earth.

So their we know the first birth came from God, when he created Adam and his help mate Eve.

We were assured, this first birth was right.

In this birth, we were so taken up in the things of the world, that we went on without noticing, the laws of the most high God.

Laws and command to live by, laws of the human life encyclopedia, which very few, or can I say some ever did take pattern.

Because of folks own agenda, and selfishness towards the most high God.

We live life without consciousnesses at times, and love towards what the Shepard has done for you, by giving us his only begotten son Jesus Christ. Jesus is crucified over and over again, day in and day out, and even though he grieve at our life style, he still stretch forth his hands towards us his children.

Giving us another chance. Thank you Lord

Here is where our second birth comes in, even though we were yet sinners, he told us by water baptism, we can be born again.(John 3-5)

God is and always will be right.

This gives you two chances, to start all over again, and repent of all your sins. The second chance, is to accept Jesus into your lives. Babies are not able to make a decision to accept Christ.

When you are grown in knowledge, you can make the right, and conscious decision, to accept Jesus Christ, and live for him, the remainder of your lives.

This is to be done speedily, because time is not promised to us, we can see today and may never see tomorrow. The world is in turmoil, with signs, and wonders everywhere. If you do see tomorrow, that means, you got another extension, and lease on life to get it right, because, twice to born and once to die.

Can you answer this question?

If you got two chances to be born again, and once to die, are you ready?

You can reflect on this next question?

When I die there is no chance to come alive again on this earth, so what will be next for you. Where will you spend eternity?

Ask yourself this, will I prefer to be in the customer care section of hell, or to be with God in and his angels in heaven.

Its up to you.

The choice is all yours.

A choice, no one can make for you.

This is something you must, and will have to do on your own.

And remember this, time is not promised to us, only God knows, the Alpha, and the omega of time.

Take this second chance to new birth seriously. You will definitely see, God is awesome, and marvelous, he is Agape (love), and his arms is outstretched towards you.

Nothing you ever do, can be so ridiculous, that he will turn his back on you.

Reach out and take his hands my people, his grip is strong, so strong that he will never let you go.

Approach the altar, of the master now. Tomorrow might be to late.

This second birth in the spirit is the greatest birth. Accept him today.

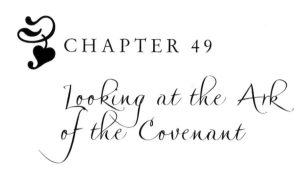

CHAPTER 49

Looking at the Ark of the Covenant

This revelation came to me on October the 10th, at 7:15 am, during morning devotion.

When you Look, at the Ark of the Covenant.

No matter how great Uzziah was, while being careful, and trying his utmost best, to save the Ark from falling, he was still killed for touching it.

God was saying to Uzziah, I have this under control Do not touch it, take your hands off. I will deal with it.

A zap of lightening surge through me, and life in general, when you are dealing with stuff, and situations in life, that is beyond your control, take your hands off totally, or he will keep you pinned down until you are ready to tap out, and let God. Until you realize that (Palms 46) is real, when it say, be still and know, that he is God. You can put a full stop upon yourself, if you do not come to your senses quickly. When you stay down to long, while holding on to the situation, you can be taken out for good, like he did to Uzziah.

This is something to shake us, into trusting in the word of God. This is the truth and God would never lie. That is why, from that day forth, David showed us, he was extremely afraid of the Lord.

The name of the place, where Uziah was struck to death, was called Perez-Uzziah, meaning the out break against Uzziah.

We sometimes need to construct, the real fear of the lion of Judah, that will get us extremely afraid like David was, he spend great time pondering on, how will the ark of the Lord come to him.

He carried the Ark into the house of Obed Odom, the Gitits, and left it their for three months. When you are not sure, of how to deal with a sudden shift of event, place it in God hands. Be it for three months like David did, or years. Before you touch it, and end up like Uzziah, embrace wisdom and keep your hands off. Be sure to, wait for the sign from God. In the mean while, remember to. Take your hands off.

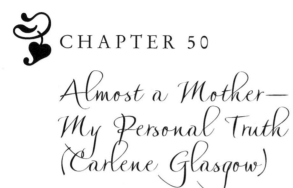

CHAPTER 50

Almost a Mother— My Personal Truth (Carlene Glasgow)

Have you ever decorated your unborn baby nursery, in your mind, but it never got to materialize?

Have you carried a beautiful baby, or in my case two babies for months, and then you miscarried them?

Have you ever given birth, then they took your baby to the incubator, where she lived for three days and then she die?

I did! Yes I said I did.

Talk starts, and planning aired the atmosphere, of what a wonderful family you will love to have.

The wedding day is upon, us and everything is proceeding as plan, when you here the word I am pregnant. The combination of joy, fear, and a change of plan fill the air, but you proceed.

At a young age, my desire were to have a boy child first, and a girl second.

My reason may have been a bit selfish, but I wanted him to look out for his little sister.

That was my wish, and dream but God had other plans for us.

My wonderful husband and I, got married at a very young

age, and still are after 37 years. I am pregnant with our first child, and guess what, it's a boy, but little did I know, this joy will be short lived. I am now growing, and everything was good, until my husband and I attended a wedding. At the wedding, I left for the restroom, and on my way back, my feet missed a stair or two, and I stumbled. I did not take it for anything at the time. When I got back, I mentioned it to my husband, and we continued to enjoy the reception.

A few days later here comes signs, like it was time to give birth. We were alarmed, because we knew this was to early. We headed of to the hospital, and I went into labor, within a few hours, I gave birth to a 5 month old baby boy. It was to early, and he did not make it, he died.

It was a feeling of despair, after all the labor pain and all that comes along with carrying a baby, and giving birth their was nothing to show. With unstoppable flow of tears, and sadness, I was discharged from the hospital. You get home, and the smell of baby powder fills the room that was prepared for your baby. Milk occupy your breast, but no one to feed it to said I. But I shook my self off, with a heavy heart, and proceed one day at a time.

We had his name chosen already, he were to be Edward like his grand pa. He was my husband father.

The year ended, and another began, when I gave the news for a second time to my husband, yes, I am pregnant.

This time it's a girl, just as I had desired. Things were proceeding beautifully, when here it goes again. She was coming to soon. At 6 plus months, I gave birth to a bouncing baby girl who weighed around 7 pounds, she was very hairy with long limbs. They took her off to clean up, and place her in the incubator, but she did not survived, she lived for three days then died.

My God, I was distraught, and wondering why me, why us. My desire and my husband's to be a father and mother another time has just shown us a minus sign. With disbelief, and Orr filling my mouth, heart, and mind I was shaken. My doctors, and nurses had to keep a close eye on my vital signs, in getting it under control.

The strength I had within showed up. I managed to stand straight, with God help.

After we lost our son and daughter we never had any more children, and being born again believers we realize God knows best, and when he has a plan for your lives, let him have his way.

Our son would have been 37 years of age now, and our daughter would have been 36 years, of age to date.

We moved on, we have lots, and lots of nieces, nephews, cousins, god children, and young people whom we love, and they feel the same, and we appreciate them all so much. This applies to those who are not blood related also. They are all our kids.

We could have sit, and slump in a state of depression, when we realize we will not be parents to our lineage, but we did not.

I held my head high, realizing there are women on this earth, who will be parents to full quivers, and some who may never have that opportunity, we realize God plans are not ours. We are content at where we are. Our love is unshakable, and the greatest love is the love of our Lord, and savior Jesus Christ. I say to childless women, never bow your head in shame, disgrace, or regrets, you can speak of the situation but never allow it to take up ownership, and residence in your life, never allow anyone to use, or hold this mishap over your head. And never give anyone, the permission to mute your voices. Always keeping in mind, your lost can be someone else's gain. I say this, because their are lots of children, and young people, who needs a parent figure in their life, and here Is where you comes in. Never consider yourself childless, because you may not have children alive, or even given birth to any. Here me, you are, and will always be desperately needed here on earth.

Believe me.

I am living proof.

Make yourself available to share, and sow into other kids lives, and I say this with great conviction, you will feel like they are your birth children. As long as you show them 100 percent, of genuine love, it will return to you.

Love is to be shared with genuineness, not stored up.

We realize, and recognize, in life when one door closes in my case two, 10 more will be opened, and its wonderful.

We admire kids who are ambitious, real, and portrays some wonderful potentials accompanied by wonderful character. This reflects, the way our kids would have been. Never the less, we never stay glued to that picture. The days of tears was over for me, many many years ago. We serve a true and living God, and know without a doubt, his plans are perfect, and he has your life map, in his hands. God has the book of notes, on each of us. So who are we to question him.

I place my arms around you my beautiful women, and I say to you, press on, and accept what you cannot change and be content with life, while enjoying it to the fullest, acknowledging it's a privilege we are around today. You could have been snatched from this earth, at a blink of an eye, but we were left here for a purpose, and a reason.

Start thinking, while asking yourself, what is my reason, and why am I still here, and you will definitely receive your answer.

I have covered so many grounds sowing into souls young, and seasoned, blessing them all around the world, bringing a laughter to their faces, and a joy to their heart, showing love at every permitted chance I get, and I say thank you Jesus.

Childless women, I have been that woman who decorated her baby nursery over, and over in my head. Who visualize her car seat, at the back seat of her jeep, who walk through the toddler section, in the maternity stores, who touched, and test lots of prams, but they never came through to reality. And this did not hinder, nor stop me. I say thank you lord because, we do not know what could have been, only Abba Father knows.

I remove the decorated nursery from my mind, and replace it with a sign reading, mentor to others.

I remove the picture in my head, of the car-seat in my jeep, and replace it with the sign mother to the motherless.

I walk backwards, through the maternity section in the store, in my mind and replace it, with the sign that reads, hold the hands of the child that's desperate for a parent figure. The smell of baby powder no longer lingers in my nostrils. The Phantom pregnancy symptoms, has disappeared. The hurt of being childless, has taken a long walk, and here I stand.

You can do the same my wonderful women. I believe in you.

I packed up all my maternity clothes, and hand it over to those who are coming after, those who are able to keep their babies, and I sow into those, who are now walking the road I walk. Those who are now sitting on a chair, day and night by the incubator, refusing to leave to get a shower, praying passionately, because their baby came before the appointed time, and are now crying hysterically. I sow into them as much as I can, because I am the living proof, of a woman who, almost became a mother.

I am that woman, who threw up for months, as she held her stomach.

I am that woman who tummy got stretch marks of all description.

I am that woman, who craved weird food.

I am that woman who's hormones moved, like a kite in a tornado season.

I am that woman, who had swollen nose, and feet

I am that woman, who never got to burp her baby

I am that woman, who never saw her babies smiles

I am that woman who was excited to introduce her full term babies to family, and the world. I am that woman who never got the opportunity to put the sign up that reads, baby on board.

I am that woman, who never got the chance to put that onezy on, that reads parents first baby.

I am that woman, who never heard the pit a pat around the house.

I am that woman, who never herd her baby cry.

I am that woman who had her babies bag packed, but never got to use it. I am that woman, who never got to take her baby for morning walks.

I am that woman who never got to look at her babies reaction, as the birds chirp.

I am that woman who never got to hear the words, Ma Ma or Da Da

I am that woman, who never got to see her babies take their first step

I am that woman who, look at another mother cuddling her baby, while I have none.

I am that woman, who never got to put the bib on her baby, that reads I love my parents. I am that woman, who kept the picture in her mind for years, of her husband's gaze that pierce through his baby, but never got to hold them. I am that woman, who's packed baby bag, was handed to the woman, on the bed next to mine, who's baby was alive. I am that woman who, understands another childless woman. Because I walked that road.

I now placed my arms around you women, daughters, ladies, and say to you, I went through, and so can you. be strong. To the women who's babies were born into this world, I say congratulation, and to those who never had the opportunity to hold her baby, keep your head held high, keeping in mind, they are many more like you on this earth.

Avail yourself to those who may need your Wisdom, and guidance to be sown into their life.

I am that woman who almost became a mother.

Carlene Glasgow.

Much love.

CHAPTER 51

Did You Know?

You were once beautiful babies at birth.

But.

Did you know?

Did you know when you were born, you will be Rich or less fortunate?

Did you know.

Did you know, you would be born with all your body parts or some?

Did you know

Did you know you would make it up the larder to prosperity, or would you be in poverty?

Did you know

Did you know you will be child less, or have your quiver over flowing?

Did you know

Did you know you will be floating on high one day, and down the larder another day?

Did you know

Did you know your knees would be strong one day, and weak the other?

Did you know

Did you know your eye site would be 20 20 today, and dim tomorrow?

Did you know

Did you know you were a blushing bride or bride groom one day, and divorce another?

Did you know

Did you know one day you are running down a long flight of stairs with enormous energy to burn, then later on, you grown to get up one stair?

Did you know

Did you know your mouth one day is full of pearly white teeth and the next you are best friend with denture?

Did you know

Did you know, when you find the love of your life, you will be together forever?

Did you know

Did you know, you will hug everyone babies, and one day you will be childless?

Did you know

Did you know you carry a baby for months, and got a chance to view them in an incubator, but will never get the chance to hold or raise them?

Did you know

Did you know, while you were using a vacuum cleaner singing into the nozzle, using it as your microphone you will one day tour the world as a Gold and Silver Medallist recording artist?

Did you know

Did you know at one point in life you were into sports running the fields jumping the gymnastic buck, and the other day you make a move, you pull a ham string?

Did you know when the nurse hands you your adorable baby at the hospital, and you look with such love at them, that one day they will turn out to be unruly rude kids, who disrespect you to the fullest?

Did you know

Did you know when you were growing up, your destiny would lead you to be a lawyer, doctor, Prime minister etc?

Did you know

You came into the world with little, then God blessings rain upon you real good did you know?

Did you know, you were steady in your movements at one point in your life, then you start shaking in your 50's and up?

Did you know

Did you know, one day you are a part of the housekeeping staff, at a fortune five hundred company and the other day you will own it all?

Did you know

Did you know you would be rich to the max at one point, and the next day you were in line at the shelter?

Did you know

Did you know, your family home will be overflowing with family members, brothers sisters, and parents, and the next, they are all gone to their own destination in life?

Did you know

Did you know your parents, who guide you through life will one day leave this earth?

Did you know

Did you know, the loving family that grew up in the same home, will one day act like strangers to each other?

Did you know.

Did you know, in your youth you were a giver sharing and blessing others, then you start keeping your hands closed with greed, and eventually lost everything?

Did you know.

Did you know, in your youth you admired, and was in orr of what a beautiful world we lived in, and suddenly, the change became so dim, with the attitudes and hate that circles earth?

Did you know.

Did you know, you will be hungry and thirsty for God,

worshiping him and the next day you are in trail blazing mode, sharing the good news throughout the world?

Did you know

Let these references be tattooed to your minds, because life has a way of suprising twists and turns, hills and valleys, shallowness and depth, that can build you up, or destroy your lives. Let this be a daily reminder, that will pinch the consciousness of hearts, never taking life for granted. Let this be your life motto. Walk in peace. Walk in humility. Walk with thanks giving. Walk in love. Hold on tightly, and engage in combat for your marriage. Share with others. Never judge others. Lend a helping hand if you can. Let your light shine towards others, giving them the benefit of the doubt, always believing, God knows it all, and he expects us to be an example of striking magnificence. Keep in mind today can be for someone else, do you know what tomorrow holds.

Did you know?

CHAPTER 52

Who Told You?

She was gathering sticks to cook both for her, and her son their last meal, then she was getting ready to die. (1 Kings:17:7:16)

After all was said and done, you throw up your hands.

After you look in the pantry, and there was nothing left.

After your last pair of shoe bottom gave way.

After you put the car keys In the ignition, and it gave its last bup bup.

You arrive to work just to hear the words, your services are no longer required.

After you get a hurenderous report from your doctor.

After you paid your last mortgage, and there is no more finance to pay the next month, and your next destination is in the streets.

After all is said and done who told you that was your last hope in life, then you lie down and die.

Who told you!!

I am positive, is not Jehovah Jeirah word. His word is yeah and Amen!

Maybe the lame man at the pool of Bethesda said that before he took up his bed, and walk (John 5:1:15).

The blind man, at the pool of Siloam may have taught this

before he gain his site (John 9:7). Abraham might have taught so, before Isaac was born.

The Egyptians taught so, before the Red sea parted (Exodus-14:21). Elijah believe this before the raven feed him at the brook. Ruth taught so, before she got favor in Boaz field, stretching her hands to put on that beautiful ring.

Who told you that after your last meal, situation, and conditions, you will die. Not our God. He will escort you out of your condition while giving you the assurance, that even if something looks dead now, Keep faith, it will come alive again. God will reboot every dead area of your life. He will restore all that the locust, and the canker worm has eaten in Jesus name. Joel 2:25.

Send Judah up

ABOUT THE AUTHOR

Carlene Glasgow a Baptized, born again believer in Christ Jesus for over 32 years. She lives her life with this mindset, less of her and more of God. A woman of faith who is radically famished, and thirsty after Jesus Christ. Married for 37 years to her blessing, and love from God her husband Mr. Alanzo Glasgow who is also a baptized born again believer for over 32 years.

We serve God with fear, no compromising, and undiluted belief.

With humbleness never taking anything for granted. Carlene has stood on many Podium and Stage executing her assignment from God, without fear, but boldness and confidence in who is holding her hands. gold medalist winner, gospel recording artist, cosmetologist, motivational speaker, image consultant, choir director, to name a few. Carlene Glasgow has ministered in countries such as Belize City Central America, Bahamas, St. Vincent and the Grenadines, Trinidad, and the U. S. A sprinkling hearts and souls with the gospel of Jesus Christ. She served on the Board level as treasurer, and worship leader for women aglow International svg chapter. During her time of ministry, and business Carlene has been in the presence of high officials, but manage to remain grounded, and humble realizing her employer is the greatest high official under heaven and on earth. Keeping in taught her assignment, gift talent, and abilities came directly from God. While zooming in on everyday life, and the waves of wind that sometimes blows in women lives today gave me a view of their value. and untapped knowledge that is hidden within, and its screaming to come out. I felt led by the Holy Spirit to share through this book giving them the confidence motivation, and empowering, while building them up spiritually. I pray as they read the blessings of God anointing will consume them. ("Lazzara".) May God help, bless and keep you.

Printed in the United States
By Bookmasters